GALIT VENTURA-ROZE
WITH 30 INCRE

Everyday
woman's
Guide To Living Your Best Life

32 Women Share Their Wisdom

The book compilation is initiated by Everyday Woman, LLC if you would like to be a published author etc etc visit www.everydaywoman.me/book or email us at everydaywomanco@gmail.com

Red Thread Publishing LLC. 2023

Write to **info@redthreadbooks.com** if you are interested in publishing with Red Thread Publishing. Learn more about publications or foreign rights acquisitions of our catalog of books: www.redthreadbooks.com

Paperback ISBN: 978-1-955683-89-0

Ebook ISBN: 978-1-955683-88-3

Contents

Introduction

Everything starts from an idea.... The key is not to let that idea stay just as an idea.

It is hard to believe this is book 5 with over 180 authors so far. Angela and I are not slowing down any time soon with these books. Why? Because we get the pleasure of giving women an opportunity to share their story with other women. For us that is everything.

Even better, our authors are getting to know other women that they are connecting with and building a community of support and empowerment. With every book we get the pleasure of getting to know new women from all over the world. We also get the pleasure of continuing to get to know the women that choose to continue in book after book.

Everyday woman was born out of a crazy time, March 2020. Even so, it has become a community of women supporting women in their passion to do what they love. This book is no different, we meet on zoom, we network, we connect, we build relationships that empower us as individuals and together as one.

Angela and I will be creating many many more books and are excited to continue to share these amazing women with you and the world. We are always open to connect with new women and would love to have you join our FB group , or one of our other opportunities such as Everyday Woman TV.

You can learn more about us at www.everydaywoman.me and you can watch Everyday Woman TV for free at www.everydaywom antv.com or on your smart tv and if you feel called to be part of our next book make sure to visit www.everydaywoman.me/book

We are thankful for our authors and all of you that take the time to read their wonderful stories of inspiration, motivation, expertise and passion!!!

Xoxo Galit and Angela
    www.everydaywoman.me
    www.everydaywoman.me/book

Chapter One

Roll With It
By Galit Ventura-Rozen

Galit started her entrepreneur career 25+ years ago in commercial real estate. She is a Broker/Owner and has sold over $700 million in properties. She is Co Founder of Everyday Woman TV, a 24/7 inspirational online network for women by women. She is a paid professional speaker and has spoken all over Canada and the United States on the topics of leadership, effective communication, mindset and more. She works with women privately to show them how to get to 7 figures in their business through teaching the methods that she has learned through out her professional career as well as owning and starting 4 businesses. She is the author of *The Successful Woman's Mindset,* her solo book, as well as 4 books she has put together with over 140 female authors.

www.linkedin.com/in/galitventurarozen
www.instagram.com/galitventurarozen
www.facebook.com/galit.rozen.9
www.galitventurarozen.com
www.tiktok.com/@galitventurarozen

Roll With It

By Galit Ventura-Rozen

At times, it seems change is occurring in my life every single day. You would think at this point I would be accustomed to it. Friends changing, employees changing, trying new things often, traveling, speaking to different audiences and more. The truth is, change is still uncomfortable and not easy, but I do not allow that feeling to stop me from continuing every day to accept it is inevitable to grow.

In life, we often encounter unexpected challenges and changes that can throw us off balance. The key to living your best life is not about avoiding these obstacles, but rather learning to adapt and roll with the punches. In this chapter, we will explore the importance of resilience and flexibility for women in navigating the ups and downs of life. By embracing change and cultivating a mindset of adaptability, we can thrive in any circumstances and truly live our best lives.

Embracing Change:

Change is inevitable, and it is essential for personal growth and development. As women, we must learn to embrace change rather than fear it. This means recognizing that change can bring new opportunities and experiences that can enrich our lives. Whether it's a career shift, a relationship change, or a relocation, the ability to adapt to change allows us to seize new possibilities and discover our true potential.

Developing Resilience:

Resilience is the ability to bounce back from setbacks and challenges. As women, we face unique obstacles in our personal and professional lives, but resilience empowers us to overcome them. Building resilience involves cultivating a positive mindset, practicing self-care, and seeking support from our networks. By developing resilience, we become better equipped to handle adversity and maintain our well-being during difficult times.

Flexibility in Goal Setting:

Setting goals is an essential aspect of living our best lives, but it's equally important to be flexible in our pursuit of those goals. Life rarely goes exactly as planned, and clinging to specific outcomes can lead to disappointment and frustration. Instead, we should focus on setting intentions and being adaptable in our approach. By allowing ourselves the flexibility to take detours and explore new paths, we may discover unexpected opportunities that lead us towards even greater fulfillment.

Navigating Personal Relationships:

Relationships play a significant role in our overall well-being. However, they, too, require flexibility and adaptability. As we grow and change, so do our relationships with others. It's important to communicate openly, listen actively, and be willing to make adjustments to maintain healthy connections. By embracing change within our relationships, we can foster growth, deepen our connections, and create harmonious dynamics that contribute to our overall happiness.

Turning Setbacks into Opportunities:

Life is not always smooth sailing, and setbacks are inevitable. However, it is how we respond to setbacks that shapes our journey. Rather than dwelling on failures or disappointments, we can choose to view setbacks as opportunities for growth and learning. With an adaptable mindset, we can extract valuable lessons from difficult experiences, refine our approach, and ultimately achieve greater success and fulfillment.

Adapting to Career Changes:

While change is inevitable, few areas of life experience more frequent and significant changes than our careers. As women, we often face unique challenges and opportunities in the professional realm. Embracing career changes requires a combination of self-reflection, strategic planning, and a willingness to step outside our comfort zones.

It is crucial to regularly assess our career goals and aspirations. As we gain experience and evolve personally and professionally, our priorities and interests may shift. Taking the time to reflect on our passions, values, and long-term objectives can help us determine if a career change is necessary or if adjustments within our current path are required.

Next, we must engage in strategic planning to navigate career transitions successfully. This involves researching potential industries, roles, and skill sets required for the desired path. Seeking out mentors or professionals who have made similar transitions can provide invaluable guidance and insights. Networking events, industry conferences, and online communities are excellent resources for connecting with individuals who can offer advice and support during this transitional phase.

Developing new skills and knowledge is often essential when pursuing a career change. Identifying the gaps in our current skill set and seeking out opportunities to acquire new competencies is crucial. This could include enrolling in courses, attending workshops, or volunteering for projects that allow us to gain hands-on experience in the desired field. Embracing lifelong learning not only enhances our professional capabilities but also demonstrates our adaptability and commitment to personal growth.

Throughout the process of adapting to career changes, it is important to remain flexible and patient. Transitioning to a new industry or role may not happen overnight, and setbacks may occur along the way. However, viewing these setbacks as learning opportunities and staying determined to achieve our goals will ultimately propel us forward. It is through perseverance and persistence that we can overcome obstacles and continue to grow professionally.

As women, we have the power to shape our lives by embracing change and cultivating an adaptable mindset. When faced with unexpected challenges and changes, let us remember that each obstacle presents an opportunity for growth and transformation. By rolling with it, we can navigate the ups and downs of life with grace and confidence, living our best lives to the fullest.

Living your best life as a woman means embracing change, cultivating resilience, and remaining flexible in the face of challenges. By adopting an adaptable mindset, we can navigate the twists and turns of life with grace and confidence. Embracing change allows us to discover new opportunities, while resilience helps us bounce back from setbacks. Being flexible in our goal setting and adaptable in our relationships enables us to find fulfillment in all aspects of our lives. So let's roll with it, embrace change, and live our best lives to the fullest!

Some of the ways that you can implement in your life to "roll with it" are:

1. Cultivate a Growth Mindset:

To truly embrace change and adapt to life's twists and turns, it's crucial to develop a growth mindset. This mindset sees challenges as opportunities for learning and growth, rather than obstacles to be avoided. Embrace the belief that your abilities can be developed through dedication and hard work. When faced with a setback or unexpected change, ask yourself: "What can I learn from this? How can I grow stronger through this experience?" By reframing challenges in this way, you empower yourself to roll with it and come out stronger on the other side.

2. Practice Mindfulness and Acceptance:

One of the keys to rolling with life's ups and downs is to practice mindfulness and acceptance. Mindfulness involves being fully present in the moment, acknowledging your thoughts and emotions without judgment. When faced with a challenging situation, take a step back, breathe, and observe your response. By accepting the reality of the situation, you can let go of resistance and focus on finding solutions or adapting to the circumstances. Remember, acceptance doesn't mean giving up; it means acknowledging what is and taking action from there.

3. Build Resilience through Self-Care:

Resilience is the ability to bounce back from setbacks, and self-care plays a vital role in building resilience. Take care of your physical, mental, and emotional well-being to better equip yourself for navigating life's challenges. Prioritize regular exercise, nourishing meals, and quality sleep. Engage in activities that recharge and rejuvenate you, such as hobbies, spending time with loved ones, or pursuing personal interests. By investing in self-care, you cultivate the inner strength needed to roll with the punches and come out stronger.

4. Seek Support and Build a Strong Network:

No woman is an island, and seeking support from others is essential in rolling with life's challenges. Surround yourself with a strong network of supportive friends, family, mentors, or professional connections. These individuals can provide guidance, advice, and emotional support when needed. Don't be afraid to ask for help or lean on others during difficult times. Sharing your experiences and seeking input from those you trust can provide new perspectives and insights that help you navigate through challenging situations.

5. Embrace Flexibility in Goal Setting and Planning:

As women, we often have long-term goals and plans for our lives. While it's important to have direction, it's equally crucial to embrace flexibility in goal setting and planning. Recognize that circumstances may change, and unexpected opportunities may arise. Remain open to adjusting your goals and plans as necessary. This doesn't mean giving up on your dreams but rather allowing room for growth, expansion, and discovery along the way. By being flexible in your approach, you'll be better equipped to adapt to changing circumstances and seize new opportunities that align with your values and desires.

Chapter Two

Embracing Your Inner Power
By Angela Giles

Angela Giles is a Marketing Pioneer, and is a passionate communicator and mentor who is driven to help her clients become successful and effective in their fields. With nearly 20 years of experience in business and digital marketing, she has an innate skill to connect with audiences of diverse backgrounds. She has helped over 2,000 business owners generate over $50+ million in sales during the past 20 years. Her goal for each training is that each member of the audience leaves inspired, confident, and ready to implement change.

www.angelagiles.com
www.facebook.com/AngelaKayGiles
www.instagram.com/angelaksgiles
www.linkedin.com/in/angelakaygiles

Embracing Your Inner Power

By Angela Giles

Listen up, ladies! If you think living your best life is all rainbows and unicorns, think again. As a fearless boss babe who has been slaying the Marketing and Sales game for 21 years, maintaining a fiery marriage for 25 years, and juggling three kids and three pups, I've learned through experience that it takes some serious sass to conquer it all.

Work-Life Harmony: Dancing on the Edge

Forget about that so-called work-life balance. It's a myth concocted by people who probably haven't handled a conference call while preparing school lunches and walking three dogs simultaneously. Life's a rollercoaster, and sometimes you have to hold on tight and ride that ride with flair.

Boundaries like a boss. Set clear boundaries for work and family time, and don't let anyone mess with that. When it's self care o'clock, my phone is on silent, and I'm cherishing those precious moments.

Delegation is not a weakness. Want to know the secret to being a powerhouse? Delegate, girl! Hand over those tedious tasks to your team and watch them shine. And hey, it's not just about lightening your load; it's about empowering others to rock it too.

Quality over everything. Who said you need to be everywhere all the time? Quality trumps quantity, whether it's clients, family time, or even friendships. Surround yourself with people who elevate you, not those who drain your fabulous energy.

Self-Care: Your Personal Pamper Party

Hey, beautiful, you can't conquer the world if you're running on empty. Self-care is not a luxury; it's your frickin' superpower.

Glow-up daily. Carve out time for yourself every single day. Whether it's a quick yoga flow, reading a juicy romance novel, or indulging in a relaxing bath, it's your sacred time to recharge that fierce spirit.

Boss up your health. Rocking that career and family life requires a healthy body and mind. Get moving, eat like the queen you are, and get the rest you need. It's tough, but trust me, it's worth it.

Passion ignition. Remember those hobbies you used to adore before adulthood took over? Reconnect with them! Dust off that guitar, dig out those art supplies, and make time for what sets your soul on fire.

Give Yourself Grace: Embrace Your Inner Goddess

Let's get real, darling. Life isn't all wins and confetti. We all make mistakes, and it's time to stop beating ourselves up about it.

Mess-ups are the new chic. Embrace the fumbles and failures, because they're proof you're in the game, baby! Learn from them, grow from them, and keep on dazzling the world.

Celebrate you, boo. It's time to stop downplaying your successes. Own that! Whether it's nailing a big project, acing your parenting skills, or just looking like a fierce queen, raise that glass and toast to your awesomeness.

Compassion is queen. When life throws you a curveball, give yourself some grace. We all have rough patches, but don't let them define you. You're strong, you're resilient, and you got this.

Experiencing Life: Unleashing Your Inner Wild Child

Living your best life isn't about playing it safe. Oh no, darling, it's about saying "yes" to adventure and squeezing every drop of juice from this delicious fruit called life.

Adventure awaits. Pack your bags, leave those comfort zones behind, and explore the world like the fearless goddess you are. Create memories that'll make your heart sing for years to come.

Cherish connections. Family, friends, and fur babies—they're your community. Shower them with love, laughter, and all the attention they deserve. These connections are the real treasures in life.

Bravery is a badge. Take risks, face your fears, and dare to be daring. Life's too short to play it safe. So put on your cape, and let your fierce brilliance shine!

In the end, my fierce ladies, living your best life is an art form. It takes sass, guts, and the audacity to be unapologetically YOU. Embrace the chaos, flaunt your brilliance, and show the world what a force of nature looks like.

Work-Life Harmony: The Art of Balancing Grace and Tenacity

As a fierce boss babe, you know that conquering the world isn't for the faint of heart. Balancing a thriving career, a sizzling marriage, and a bustling family can sometimes feel like walking on a tightrope. But let me tell you, it's not about finding that elusive "work-life balance" - it's about mastering the art of work-life harmony.

Setting Boundaries: Boss Babe Style

You don't have time for blurred lines. Set clear boundaries between your professional and personal life, and let the world know you mean business. When the clock strikes "me time," put that phone on silent, and relish in the moments that matter.

Delegation: Empower Yourself and Others

You're a force to be reckoned with, but even boss babes need a little help sometimes. Don't be afraid to delegate those tasks that weigh you down. Empower your team to shine and make room for your own brilliance to soar.

Quality Trumps Quantity: Surround Yourself with Fabulousness

You're not interested in anything mediocre. Whether it's clients, friends, or family time, it's all about quality over quantity. Surround yourself with those who elevate and inspire you, and watch your life become a dazzling masterpiece.

Self-Care: Your Secret Superpower

You're the queen of your kingdom, and every queen needs some pampering. Self-care isn't a luxury; it's your secret superpower.

Glow-Up: Unleash the Radiant Goddess Within

Honey, you were born to shine. Carve out time each day for self-love and care. Whether it's a power-packed yoga session, reading a steamy romance novel, or indulging in a spa-like bath, make self-care a non-negotiable part of your routine.

Boss Up Your Health: Fuel Your Fire

You're on a mission, and that takes a fit and fabulous body and mind. Move it, fuel it, and get the rest you need to slay like the fierce queen you are. It may be tough, but trust me, you're worth every bit of effort.

Ignite Your Passion: Rediscover Your Spark

Before the world told you who you should be, you had dreams and passions that lit up your soul. It's time to reclaim them. Dust off that old guitar, grab those forgotten art supplies, and indulge in the passions that make your heart sing.

Give Yourself Grace: Embrace the Beauty of Imperfection

Life isn't about perfection - it's about embracing the perfectly imperfect you. Darling, you're not defined by your mistakes. Embrace them as opportunities to learn, grow, and dazzle the world even brighter.

Mess-Ups are the New Chic: Celebrate Your Journey

You're a work in progress, and that's what makes you fabulous. Celebrate your fumbles and failures as milestones on your journey to greatness. Embrace the process, and never forget that you're in the game, baby!

Own Your Awesomeness: Toast to Your Triumphs

It's time to take the spotlight and own your successes. Whether you've rocked a big project, aced those parenting skills, or simply looked like a fierce queen, raise that glass and toast to the badass that you are.

Compassion is Queen: Embrace Your Inner Goddess

Life can be tough, but so are you. When challenges arise, show yourself some compassion. You're strong, you're resilient, and you've got the power to conquer whatever comes your way.

Experiencing Life: Unleashing Your Inner Wild Child

Life's wild, and so are you. Take risks, face your fears, and let your fierce brilliance shine. Put on that cape and embrace your inner superhero, because you've got the power to make life extraordinary.

Adventure Awaits: Embrace the Unknown

Pack your bags, leave those comfort zones behind, and explore the world like the fearless goddess you are. Adventure is your birthright, and it's time to claim it.

Cherish Connections: Love, Laugh, and Live

Your tribe is everything. Shower your family, friends, and fur babies with love, laughter, and all the attention they deserve. These connections are the real treasures in life.

Bravery is Your Badge: Dare to Be Daring

Life's too short to play it safe. So put on your cape and let your fierce brilliance shine!

In the end, my fierce ladies, living your best life is an art form. It takes sass, guts, and the audacity to be unapologetically YOU. Embrace the chaos, flaunt your brilliance, and show the world what a force of nature looks like. Work-life harmony, self-care, and embracing your inner power are your secret weapons on this wild ride. So, grab your tiara and unleash that inner queen because this is your time to shine!

mic drop

Chapter Three

Who's That Woman In The Mirror
By Coree Sullivan

C oree Sullivan has a heart to help those who've gone through the painful experience of divorce find the deep inner healing that will help them thrive in their new lives. She is a certified Life Coach specializing in the unique issues that rise out of the pain divorce causes us.

Coree is the author of the best selling book *Destiny After Divorce* as well as a much sought after Speaker, as she provides great insight along with humor in her presentations. She resides in Windsor, Co., has 2 married daughters, 6 grandchildren and 4 great-grandchildren.

www.linkedin.com/in/coree-sullivan-8851a724

www.instagram.com/coreesullivan

www.facebook.com/thisrestoredheartministries

www.CoreeSullivan.com

Who's That Woman In The Mirror

By Coree Sullivan

There she was, intently looking back at me. She was the woman in the mirror.

"Who is this woman...I mean who REALLY is this woman?" She seemed to ask me. What's the expression on her face telling me? The reflection made my heart ponder the question at a deeper level.

The look in her eyes was that of a wise warrior, yet they had compassion for me. They had a tinge of a smile to soften the sternness in them. Where did all of this come from? Those eyes went to such a depth that my spirit struggled to grasp it.

It had been a long time since I had really had a real, close, deep, look into the eyes of the woman in the mirror. I began to take stock of the woman looking back at me.

She had developed some wrinkles around her eyes that indicated she had laughed and smiled a lot. Along with those smile lines came some sweet memories of times with her children, as they were growing up, followed by how they had become amazing moms themselves, and a sense of pride came into her eyes.

The times of laughter with her grandchildren and great grandchildren started to come to the forefront of her mind and the lines began to crinkle with the memories of wonderful, fun times with them. Some were very recent, but had already been filed away in the happy memory file.

The furrow between her eyebrows was deeper than she liked, but spoke to the determination and sense of purpose she conducted herself with, day in and day out. It reminded her of times she had serious decisions to make and the thought process that she went through in order to be able to make those decisions, or take the next steps, so she could move forward in her life.

The wrinkles on her upper lips were the most annoying to her.

But she realized that when she smiled, they disappeared. So, she made a mental note to smile more.

However, the deep intensity of her gaze was filled with a knowing that came from being a long time warrior, tempered with the maturity that comes through the balance of wisdom and compassion. That was the thing that kept my gaze connected to her.

It was at that moment that she realized that the woman in the mirror was an outward reflection of a beautiful, capable woman who had not only survived the day in – day out journey of life, but had learned to thrive through it all! She had some battle scars, but all in all, the woman looking back at me in the mirror truly was thriving.

She had learned that the core of her survival was the foundation of her strength coming from the time she spent in the morning to connect and meditate. It was a time to quiet her mind and spirit so she could connect with Jesus in order to come from a place of strength throughout her day. A place where her wisdom took shape without the distractions of the day.

Being a woman in today's world takes great strength, wisdom and compassion no matter what we do in our day-to-day lives. Some mornings it takes strength just to get out of bed and face the day.

We, as women, wear a lot of hats throughout the day. I remember many times having to get up and get my girls off to school with the thought in the back of my mind of how I was going to go into work and ask for a raise that day? I knew my review was coming up and I had a number in mind that I wanted that raise to be.

I spent some time sitting in my car, after dropping my girls off, envisioning myself sitting in front of my supervisor, and how I was going to present my request. I had armed myself with my accomplishments that included improving the company's bottom line and earned our branch an award from the owner of the company.

I also had a list of new customers that were now buying from us as a result of my marketing efforts. And the grand kicker was, I had done this with a smaller staff than anyone who had held my position before.

My confidence level was high when I walked into my supervisor's office that day. To my surprise, he had already reviewed the stats from my department and gave me a great review. You can imagine my response of joy when he gave me a raise that was more than I was going to ask for!

I thought back to the days and weeks of meetings with my team and the goals we had set to attain on a weekly, then monthly basis, so that we could hit our overall goals. It had all happened through the foundation of smaller goals to be able to reach the big goals. And it was accomplished by being our best each and every day.

With all that in mind, I have learned that a great outcome starts with a strong foundation. That foundation for me was my quiet time in the morning to have the clarity to not only get through the day but to take a few more steps toward my end goals. During that time, I also sought wisdom for my daily, weekly and monthly tasks.

I started with a vision for the type of life I wanted to live and how I wanted to provide for my daughters. From there, I set my daily, weekly and monthly goals. I sought continued wisdom in my quiet time to achieve these goals. Sometimes I found I needed to modify my goals when things went faster or slower due to outside influences or unforeseen obstacles that came up. Or sometimes, the goals changed because they no longer were as important and something else took their place.

It was important to not set things in stone because the journey of life has many twists and turns. Shortly after my raise and glowing review, a new supervisor came in and set the bar even higher than my former supervisor. He made it clear that there was no negotiation in the goals he had set either. So, my team and I had to go back and adjust our daily, weekly and monthly goals to meet the ones he had set.

We missed hitting his goals in the first quarter, which he wasn't very happy about. As a result, we had to go back and adjust our goals again so that we wouldn't come up short in the following quarter. We were able to hit them for that quarter, which resulted in bonuses for us, but the goal was pushed out even further after that.

I've discovered throughout my life that goals are always going to move and our success depends on how well we adjust. We struggle with self-doubt, negativity and stress when things happen to us, or at least I certainly have. That in turn sometimes leads us to want to just give up, pick up our briefcases and find a new game to play in. But we were in that game for a reason. Through that game I learned new skills as well as had more wisdom and clarity about my goals.

In my past, I've learned more about the journey and how to navigate through overcoming obstacles than I have ever learned any other way. I still am learning about how to overcome obstacles and struggles in order to accomplish my goals.

My ultimate vision has changed somewhat as well. I've learned that sometimes I need to open my mind to new skills and new tools in order to accomplish the ultimate goal of the vision I carry for my future.

My quiet morning times provide a great foundation for the day but need to be fortified with 'self-care' time in order to avoid burnout and negativity. I've learned I need to be compassionate with myself, as well as others who have come alongside me on my journey.

Sometimes we forget to be compassionate with ourselves but offer great compassion to others. I had to learn to not neglect myself.

As I look in the mirror at the woman looking back at me, I realize that the depth in her eyes came from who she is becoming through her journey on a daily basis. It isn't about the goals, the vision, even though that was the driving force behind it all. It was, and still is about the journey and the memories made on this journey.

However, now the woman in the mirror is wiser, and more beautiful, confident, and compassionate than ever before. Wrinkles and all. It's through her eyes that I see the beauty, grace and ability to be an everyday woman, living her best life ever, one day at a time.

Chapter Four

Triumph Over Tragedy
By Yolla Alsabagh

Yolla Alsabagh is a formidable force in the insurance industry, wielding expertise as a licensed life insurance and Medicare agent in multiple states. With a remarkable track record, she has established herself as a sought-after trainer, empowering agents in selling final expense life insurance coverage with finesse and confidence.

Determined to make a difference, Yolla's career journey has been an inspiration to peers and clients alike. Her passion for the industry, combined with her in-depth knowledge, has catapulted her into the spotlight, earning her well-deserved recognition. Being voted into Real Vegas Magazine's "Women Who Wow" category for four consecutive years is a testament to her unwavering dedication and the impact she has on her field.

Yolla's training sessions are characterized by her vibrant energy and commitment to excellence. Agents under her guidance benefit from her wealth of experience, gaining insights that elevate their professional capabilities. Her unique approach to understanding client needs and tailoring solutions has earned her a loyal following and numerous success stories.

Beyond her professional achievements, Yolla remains grounded and true to herself. She cherishes her time with family and friends, embracing the joy of travel and the thrill of discovering new cultures. Balancing her career with a passion for photography, she captures moments that speak to the essence of life's beauty.

As Yolla continues her journey of impact and influence, her story exemplifies a woman who lives her best life unapologetically. Empowered by her accomplishments, she sets her sights on even greater heights, eager to leave a lasting legacy in the insurance industry and beyond. With each day, Yolla illuminates the path for others, embodying the spirit of passion, dedication, and a relentless pursuit of success.

www.instagram.com/lebanesediva79
www.vipinsuranceadvocates.com

Triumph Over Tragedy

By Yolla Alsabagh

Life has an extraordinary way of molding us through trials and tribulations, and my journey has been no exception. You see, I am no different than you are, I have had my fair share of grief and loss, character defining moments and growth. However, as I sit here and write this chapter today, I am filled with gratitude that I get to share a little about my story with you. My hope is that I get to inspire at least one woman to live a life that is also unapologetically hers.

My family immigrated from Lebanon when I was a child. Being Lebanese American is a beautiful fusion of two worlds, where my heritage and cultural roots intertwine with the rich tapestry of America. I carry the traditions, language, and customs of my ancestors, connecting me to a vibrant and diverse community that spans continents. I embrace the values of hospitality, family bonds, and a deep appreciation for art, music, and cuisine that have been passed down through generations in Lebanon. Yet, I also cherish the opportunities and freedoms that America offers, allowing me to pursue my dreams and carve my unique path. I have proudly broken several glass ceilings for my family and culture and I look forward to many more positive milestones.

A few years ago, I was honored to be included as an author in "The Successful Woman's Mindset. 21 Journeys to Success" where I talked about my struggle with infertility and the painful loss of a child.Losing a child was an indescribable heartache that shattered my world. The pain was all-consuming, leaving me feeling empty and broken.Infertility was a silent struggle that left me feeling isolated and alone. Each negative pregnancy test felt like a blow to my hopes and dreams of motherhood. But as the months turned into years, I learned to shift my perspective. Infertility became an unexpected teacher, teaching me patience, acceptance, and the art of surrendering to the universe's timeline. It was amidst the grief, I found an unfathomable well of resilience within myself.

As I confronted the reality of infertility, I learned to embrace motherhood in different forms. I nurtured the relationships with the children in my life. I met and married the love of my life who had a child before we met and I am happy being her bonus mom (No steps in this family).

I am an aunt to the most incredible young men and women. I found joy in showering love upon these young souls God blessed me with and I enjoy celebrating the unique connection we share. I am proud of each one of my kiddos, my nieces and nephews who are also making their mark on history throughout the world.

Long before infertility was a chapter, obesity and health problems had also dominated my life for years. In a world seemingly obsessed with appearances, I found myself navigating through the shadows cast by society's judgments, carrying the weight of obesity on my shoulders. For years, I battled the relentless grip of excess weight, feeling trapped in a body that never really felt like my own. The struggle was not just physical but emotional, as I grappled with self-doubt, shame, and a longing for acceptance.

Like a mountain looming before me, the challenge of battling obesity seemed insurmountable. The journey towards reclaiming my health was a treacherous one, riddled with setbacks and moments of despair. The path was laden with temptations, and old habits lingered like deep-rooted vines, threatening to ensnare my progress.

That battle ended with a choice—the choice to confront the truths I had been avoiding. With every step towards change, I found myself shedding more than just pounds; I shed the layers of denial that had shielded me from the reality of my health. I looked within, acknowledging the patterns that led me to this point, and embraced the courage to confront the root causes.

As I ventured into uncharted territory, I sought guidance from healthcare professionals, nutritionists, and opted for gastric sleeve surgery. That transformation provided me with a compass, guiding me towards a healthier lifestyle. With newfound knowledge, I began to make small, sustainable changes to my diet and exercise routine.

Instead of a quick fix, I adopted a mindset of long-term wellness—a commitment to nurturing my body and spirit.

Yet, the journey was not without its challenges. There were moments of stumbling, moments when I questioned my strength to continue. But with each fall, I learned to rise again, drawing upon the resilience that had been dormant within me. I reminded myself that progress was not always linear, and setbacks were an opportunity for growth, not a sign of failure.

Embracing the journey towards conquering obesity involved more than just physical transformation; it required a shift in my perception of self-worth. I learned that my value as a person was not defined by the number on the scale. The battle was not just about losing weight but about gaining self-acceptance, self-love, and a deep appreciation for my body's capabilities.

With time, the pounds began to shed, revealing a newfound sense of freedom. I relished the moments when I could climb a flight of stairs without gasping for breath, or when I discovered the joy of movement through exercise. Each milestone was a victory, reminding me of the progress I had made and the strength that had emerged from within.

As the journey continued, I discovered a newfound passion for cooking nutritious meals, transforming the kitchen into a canvas of colors and flavors. Eating mindfully became an act of self-nourishment, not just physically but emotionally. Food was no longer a source of comfort or escape; it became a celebration of life and vitality.

Through all these battles, I not only discovered the power of self-love but also the importance of self-compassion. I forgave myself for past mistakes and treated each day as a fresh opportunity to make healthier choices. I learned to silence the inner critic and replaced it with a voice of encouragement and positivity.

As I look back on the path I have walked, I see the mountains I have conquered and the valleys I have emerged from.

Living my best life required me to embrace vulnerability,

acknowledging the pain and fears that had long been hidden within. I learned to open my heart to the difficult emotions, allowing myself to grieve, to cry, and to be vulnerable without judgment. In my vulnerability, I found the strength to heal and grow.

My challenges didn't define me; they molded me into a person of strength and resilience. I learned to rise above the hardships, transcending the limitations I once believed defined me. My journey towards living my best life was not a linear path but a meandering road that led me to self-acceptance and empowerment.

Living my best life was not about reaching a destination of perfection; it was about embracing the everyday magic in every step of the journey. It was about finding beauty in the simple moments, cherishing the love of family and friends, and embracing the imperfections that made me uniquely human.

Living my best life unapologetically is an embrace of my true self, free from the shackles of societal expectations and judgments. It is about honoring my passions, dreams, and values, even if they deviate from the norm. With each step, I walk confidently, celebrating my uniqueness and the beauty of my individuality. Unapologetically, I take risks and embrace the journey of self-discovery, unafraid of making mistakes along the way. This path is a celebration of authenticity, where I let go of the need for approval and live according to my own compass. Living my best life unapologetically empowers me to stand tall and embrace the fullness of my being, painting my life's canvas with bold strokes of courage, joy, and unwavering self-acceptance.

As this chapter of my life unfolds, I stand at the intersection of resilience and self-discovery, fully embracing the art of living my best life. The journey has been one of triumphs and trials, a dance of light and shadow that has sculpted the person I have become. Through the depths of loss, infertility, obesity, and the pursuit of success, I have learned to cherish the everyday magic that surrounds me.

Living my best life is not about perfection, for I have come to embrace the beauty of imperfections and the lessons they teach. It is about unapologetically being myself, celebrating the unique tapestry of my heritage, my passions, and my dreams. The battles I have faced have gifted me with resilience, courage, and the strength to overcome obstacles that once seemed insurmountable.

As I continue on this journey, I hold gratitude in my heart for the connections I have formed, the support I have received, and the growth that has unfolded within me. Each chapter of my story has woven together to create a narrative of authenticity, self-love, and empowerment.

Living my best life is not a destination but an ever-evolving adventure, where I nurture my dreams, embrace vulnerability, and seek the beauty in the ordinary. I walk with confidence, knowing that the trials I have overcome have sculpted me into a person capable of conquering any mountain that lies ahead.

As I turn the page to the next chapter, I step forward with anticipation and curiosity, for the journey towards living my best life is a lifelong odyssey. With each step, I celebrate the person I am becoming, knowing that my story is still unfolding, and the best is yet to come.

Chapter Five

I Dare You to Care
by Michelle Weihman

M ichelle is an award-winning nurse leader, #1 Bestselling author and puppy rescuer.

However, nothing came easy for her. A high-school dropout, married at 16, Michelle's future did not look bright.

But with faith in God, determination, and belief in herself she overcame the obstacles and challenges to fulfill her destiny.

Today as a speaker, coach and thought leader she wants to instill more humanity in leadership and empower a new breed of leadership for the future.

www.linkedin.com/mwlite/in/michelle-renee-weihman-rn-02a45196

www.instagram.com/michellereneeweihman

m.facebook.com/Michelle-Renee-Weihman-RN-114788313690124/

www.Michellereneeweihman.com

I Dare You to Care

by Michelle Weihman

It seems to me that over the past few years people have forgotten the art of caring. As we rush through our busy day, we communicate through emails and texts, losing virtually all the human touch that our body not only desires, but our soul needs. In today's fast-paced and demanding world, burnout has become a prevalent issue, affecting individuals across various careers. Burnout can leave us feeling exhausted, overwhelmed, and detached from the things that once brought us joy. In this chapter, we will explore the causes and symptoms of burnout, as well as practical strategies to overcome it and restore a sense of balance in our lives. By prioritizing self-care, setting boundaries, and cultivating resilience, we can navigate the challenges of burnout and reclaim our well-being.

So I ask you, have you experienced any of the following?

- Headache
- Fatigue
- Cynicism
- Irritability
- Insomnia
- Disillusionment
- Apathy
- Hopelessness

If so, you may be experiencing burnout. Burnout is defined as "a state of emotional, physical, and mental exhaustion that results from prolonged stress and frustration. It is a common phenomenon among those who work long hours, experience high levels of job demand, and have little control over their work environment." As a nurse of nearly 30 years, I know a bit about burnout.

Year of the Nurse

The year 2020 was Florence Nightingale's 200th birthday. You may be wondering who Florence Nightingale is and why we should care when her 200th birthday was. Florence Nightingale is considered the Founder of Modern Nursing. She is known for her pioneering efforts to improve sanitation in hospitals and healthcare for all. Thanks to her we discovered the importance of hand hygiene and sanitation in preventing disease and reducing mortality.

Not only was 2020 Florence Nightingale's 200th birthday it was also supposedly the Year of the Nurse! As I said, I have been a nurse for a LONG time, and it is finally our year! Okay, so just in case you don't remember, let me remind you a bit about 2020. This was the start of the pandemic, Corona Virus, COVID, whatever you want to call it, it was the year that nurses were praised for being heroes and accused of making the problem worse. If this was how the Year of the Nurse was planned, NO THANK YOU!

My Call to Nursing

I always knew I was going to be a nurse. When other girls were playing house, I was playing nurse. I gave my dolls shots, bandaged their boo-boos, I took their temperature, I gave them medicine. I was the girl who took students to the nurse when they were injured on the playground. I always knew I was a nurse. Nursing is more than a job, it's a calling.

Although nursing has been one of my biggest blessings, it has also presented me with the opportunity to be a blessing to more than just my patients. You see, being a nurse is hard; we literally have people's lives in our hands. Meanwhile, we have doctors, family members, administration, even government agencies all "managing" the care we provide. Nurses are caring for more patients, sicker patients, with less resources. This can and does lead to burnout.

What is Burnout and How Does It Affect You?

Burnout may not be a medical diagnosis but those affected by it can have physical symptoms, mental distress, and emotional exhaustion. It is characterized by feelings of cynicism, detachment, and reduced feeling of personal accomplishment which can lead to decreased job satisfaction, increased absenteeism, and turnover.

In nursing, burnout can have serious consequences for patient care, as it may affect the quality of care provided, increase the risk of medical errors, and compromise patient safety.

But burnout can and does affect more than just nursing. Burnout is present in every field. As you read this, even if you are not a nurse you will realize how you are affected by burnout, directly and indirectly.

A few of the causes of burnout include lack of recognition and support, not feeling heard, not receiving clarity of expectations, and pressure to be even more productive. The pandemic led to a situation where nurses felt these things were stacked high. The patients were sicker and there were more of them. The nurses themselves were getting sick and couldn't come to work. All of this led to higher patient to nurse ratios with sicker patients. The leadership team was trying to accommodate, to hire more staff, to utilize "travelers" to no avail, and the patients kept coming. Burnout in nursing was at an all-time high.

Burnout is like a leaky faucet; it drains the employee, and it costs the employer a lot of money. According to the Journal of Occupational and Environmental Medicine the cost of nurse turnover due to burnout in the United States is approximately $9 billion per year. In addition to the cost of turnover, there is the cost of preventable medical errors which cost the United States as much as $400 billion per year! While burnout is well known in the healthcare setting, this is not the only place it lives. Burnout knows no limitations.

Burnout can show up as mood swings, physical symptoms like headaches or insomnia, decreased productivity, or social withdrawal.

Spot these signs in someone? Start by having an empathetic conversation, encourage self-care, and offer help. Importantly, respect their process - healing from burnout needs time, understanding, and patience.

I wish I could say that this can be fixed on the "corporate" level but burnout is a multidimensional problem that needs to be "fixed" on both a corporate and personal level. We all need to fix burnout.

We need to be watching out for each other and if we see someone struggling, we should pull them aside and ask if they are okay. We need to take our "young" under our wing, guide them, care for them, mentor them. Many of our "young" nurses went to school during the pandemic and did not get the hands-on training that one would expect.

The Prescription for Burnout

And we need to take time for **S.E.L.F.C.A.R.E.**

- **S—Stillness** Take time every day for stillness, silence, meditation, or prayer. Take time every day, even if it is just 3 minutes to be still and know.
- **E—Energy** Take a moment every day to create energy (even when you don't feel like it) Create an energetic force around yourself. DANCE PARTY!!
- **L—Love** We truly do not know what others are going through. Show them LOVE, not because they deserve it, but because YOU deserve it!
- **F—Fearlessness** Be Freaking FEARLESS! Do something that scares you. Write that book, get up on stage, talk to your neighbor. Growth does not come from complacency.
- **C—Compassion** Show compassion to the living souls around you. The Dali Lama says that compassion is a

necessity, not a luxury. Without it humanity cannot survive.

- **A—Affirmation** What we tell ourselves is what we believe. I can tell you positive things but if your self-talk is negative, what I say means little to nothing. Create and repeat affirmations daily. "I am worthy. I am enough. I am unstoppable. I am deserving of good health, happiness, love, and peace."
- **R—Receive** Open your palms and receive what is given to you, including compliments. We are taught that it is better to give than to receive. Stop taking away the other person's joy in giving. Just say "Thank you".
- **E—Empower** Hurt people hurt people. Empowered people empower people. If you don't feel empowered where you are, empower yourself. Take the initiative. Belief in yourself. And if you have trouble believing in yourself, know that I believe in you!

Will You Take the Dare?

In a world that's often too busy and impersonal, let's rekindle the art of caring, for others and ourselves. Burnout is a sign of the times, but it's not an inevitability. Recognizing it in ourselves and others is the first step. Actively taking measures to combat it - by embracing self-care, setting boundaries, cultivating resilience - is the next. And remember, caring is cool. It's human. It's a language that speaks directly to the heart. So here's my challenge to you: I dare you. I dare you to prioritize yourself, to care for your colleagues, to become more resilient, to beat burnout. I dare you to care - not because it's easy, but because it's worth it. And as you step into this dare, remember that the first person you need to care for is you. Let's make caring the norm, not the exception. You in?

Chapter Six

Be Your Incredible Self
A. Garcia

M s. Garcia has a tenacious attitude towards empowering others. Over the past 35 years she has navigated through domestic violence, privacy, safety, vulnerability, and the mindset to endure personal adverse events in life. Her survival of a double attempted homicide while 8 months pregnant (by the father) and the desperation to survive became the catalyst to the founding of Be Your Incredible Self while achieving an undisputed outlook of extreme independence. Although it is a natural trauma driven response, Garcia will openly admit, it became her self sabotaging trait like an addiction.

Through years of boots on the ground wisdom, with a God

fearing heart and purpose driven life, at her own risk, Garcia shares her personal story and recently established a nonprofit to Confront Domestic Violence both in real time and by challenging current policies.

Her personal journey of Post Traumatic Growth has led Garcia to dedicating her life in developing transformational programs and various forms of coaching to bring emotional awareness, positive intelligence and clear cut confidence to experience Post Traumatic Growth and take action to live a more satisfying life.

www.linkedin.com/posts/agarcia247_beyourincredibleself-domesticviolence-activity-6957426297660731392-1ohV

www.instagram.com/beyourincredibleself

www.facebook.com/beincredible

www.beyourincredibleself.com

www.everydaywomantv.com/tv_shows/confronting-domestic-violence

Be Your Incredible Self

By A. Garcia

The ability to live your best life, what does that really mean or even look like? Well, we all have the ability to live it! Now, before I start breaking that down, I invite you to first identify what your definition of Living Your Best Life truly is. Take a few minutes to marinate on that, think about it through your layers, down to your core. It's not a knee-jerk answer and I guarantee you; we all have different answers. As a woman, mother, daughter, sister, wife, aunt, best friend, leader, and so on, we leave a footprint and an impact on so many people around us. Yet, the only one that truly knows you to the core, your sincere happiness, your genuine coping challenges, and your outlook on life - is you! That's why this topic is so important to everyday women like you and me. No matter what other people see, hear, or perceive of you; it's what's actually going on within you that determines if, in fact, you are living your best life. In this brief chapter, I am going to provoke thought and share multiple strategies I have personally learned, applied, developed, and deployed to this day that allows me to maintain the required mindset to live my best life.

First and foremost, let's talk about where you live every second of the day regardless of where you might be in the physical sense. If you're still wondering what I might be talking about, I'm referring to your head! That's right, no matter where you are physically, or how many times you move, you live in your head. So having your mental house in order is an absolute must if you truly want to start living your best life. Of course, there are several levels to this, I will touch on some and emphasize on others to help get you on your way immediately. After all, you deserve it! Once you accept you are the only thing you can control, and you start letting go of trying to control things outside of yourself, you will be better equipped with the tools needed to:

- Determine the way your best self wants to navigate through the day
- Know exactly who needs you on your 'A' Game
- Identify what may pull you from your 'A' Game
- Clarify how will you mitigate potential distractions

If you can create a morning routine identifying the above, you are setting yourself up for success off the bat! Although I mentioned routine, I highly encourage you to make this a conditioned habit for yourself. If you're asking how long that will take, research shows anywhere from 28 – 70 days. Being consistent is key! As your brain is the largest muscle in your body, like clockwork your behavior will chase what's on your brain. I'm sure you heard the term by T. Robbins, "Energy flows where the attention goes". When your mind is uncluttered, it enables you to be clearer about who you are, your purpose, why you're doing what you're doing, and the direction you are committed to going. Did I mention how GREAT this feels? If you're at the place of being overwhelmed or feeling like everything you're a part of is chaotic and nothing you've done previously is working, then get started on the above 4 simple thought-provoking tasks right away, in the morning! Daily personal growth is a sure-fire way to live your best life and you will be amazed at how much it can improve your everyday experience in your pursuit of genuine happiness.

Let's face it, you are an influencer whether you recognize and or accept it or not. Someone is always watching, listening, learning, judging, absorbing, perceiving, you name it – you're making a difference in lives! What an awesome way to live your best life – leaving a solid imprint of who you are, what you represent, and for some, a bona fide legacy. If you're reading this, I know you believe in yourself which means you can create the energy needed to level up a notch. What do I mean by that? What if you could motivate and push others to a higher standard of excellence? What would you start with first? How would you lead by example? The answers to those questions will help you gain more clarity about your character and the influence you have on yourself and those around you. Staying intentional with your actions, making meaningful choices, and being confident in your commitments is a solid foundation to build on. The more your actions back up your positive beliefs, and you feel like your contributions make a meaningful difference, the more emotionally connected you are with your 'why' which raises a great sense of necessity. All of which are additional layers to living your best life!

Has anyone ever encouraged you to consider how 'the greatest opportunities in your life right now are the ones you are most grateful for'? Take a moment to consider that and identify what you're grateful for in your life and why. Capture them and expand in more detail, layer by layer until you see the bigger picture. This will bring additional awareness and confidence in your pursuit of these opportunities. Ask yourself what makes you feel most confident and say it out loud. As silly as this may sound, take yourself to the mirror and say it to yourself right there. Literally, look yourself in the eyes, and tell yourself what makes you confident, repeat it a few times, have a heart-to-heart conversation with yourself. Mirror neurons are something I have studied and applied for years; it is a real thing!! Please do this exercise regularly. Again, consistency is key so 3-4 times a day will soon become a solid tool to turn your confidence 'ON' when it is most needed. Always say what you mean when you're talking to yourself and definitely when in the mirror!

Alright, let's visit when time hits near the end of the day for you. I like to call this moment 'The Pulse Check.' Where you take a moment for yourself to reflect on yourself and your day. Setting an alarm at the same time nightly will allow you to start creating a routine for this great moment with yourself. Here are some questions of reflection for you to implement into your routine:

- Was I confronted with anything that challenged my ability to be my best self today?
- Did I manage my energy well? Both mentally and physically?

- Was there any situation I could have made even better?
- What happened today that I really appreciated?

Sorry, not sorry, but have you recognized that you are your biggest critic? Are you a bigger critic when things are going really well for you? Do you feel yourself experiencing a form of imposter syndrome? Unfortunately, we all have a tendency to listen to our negative inner critic that can sometimes become our heightened personal self sabotager. Whether it's stripping confidence, energy, or relationships, if you don't learn how to intercept it, you won't be able to control it. I mean, if someone else told you the negative things you tell yourself, how would you respond? Would you consider that a healthy relationship? Believe me, the challenge it requires to navigate through Emotional Intelligence and Positive Intelligence (EQ/PQ) is more than worth the outcome! Most of us have faced devastating life situations that have changed our opinions, boundaries, confidence, awareness, and so many other things. When having the mindset to live your best life, it boils down to how you're coping, how you're optimizing your well-being to feel your best, and what you're doing to stay energetic and strong!

As you apply the above exercises daily, and it becomes a conditioned habit, you'll start cultivating a higher sense of joy and positive attitude naturally resulting in authentically living your best life. After all, it's your headspace that you reside in, so keeping the most positive outlook, identifying the greatness that came out of a rough life situation, and acknowledging that you came out stronger and smarter is sheer resilience!! Dealing with the world's stress is more than enough. Let the doubts of the outside uncontrollable circumstances go and be your biggest cheerleader, and watch your confidence grow as you tap into your hobbies, your adventures, your vibrancy, and your stamina!

Chapter Seven

Your Empowered Life
By Tracy Nosal

Tracy Nosal also known as The Renegade Mentor is an Intuitive Transformational Coach. Tracy's life's work is assisting High Achieving Women break through any barriers that have kept them stuck, frustrated and unfulfilled.

Her 30 plus years of customer relations with a degree in Applied Science has come full circle to the metaphysical field. She has been trained and certified in many healing arts which she utilizes with her coaching clients. Tracy quickly identifies the blindspots that are stored in the subconscious mind and teaches her clients how to live into lasting change which lasts long after the sessions have ended.

Tracy's programs empower women and teach how energetic alignment truly work so you can create the life you know you are meant to live.

www.linkedin.com/in/tracy-nosal-6ab66624a
www.instagram.com/renegade_mentor
www.facebook.com/Renegade Mentor

Your Empowered Life

By Tracy Nosal

People think you have to be monetarily rich to live your best life. Actually, I think the secret is being happy in how you live.

How do you show up in your life? Are you happy, or stressed?

It's your predominant thoughts that guide your life. Being grateful brings more great situations into your life. So you may think, but I don't always feel positive and that's okay. This is your opportunity to evaluate what is really on your mind.

Those thoughts you tend to push off to the side are the ones that are stored in your subconscious mind that actually run a frequency. This frequency is what is actually running the show in your life. Your old patterns of emotions become your current cycle in life. When you elevate your life by releasing outdated emotions and behavior patterns, a new life will emerge.

It takes practice to stay happy, or at least neutral. Remember when you make a choice to change how you feel, it needs time to become a habit. When you practice being neutral versus being reactive, then situations in your life will begin to change. The work is done from within.

Your empowered life is knowing who you are at a soul level! So, how well do you know yourself? I know you may think that is a silly question, but have you ever really gone within? What are your hopes, and more importantly, your FEARS? What is it that you prefer not to think about? Have you been ignoring those parts of you that you don't want to face? Freeing these hidden emotions you've been busy denying is the very thing that will set you free!

It's time to set down the weight of the burdens you've been carrying. Have you ever noticed that when you stop worrying, everything starts to work in your favor? That is due to a shift in your thinking, which shifts your personal frequency. Hence when you are positive, life feels great, and when you are negative, everything seems to be a struggle.

It's your mind that swings back and forth between having faith and allowing everything to line up versus how life is when you are constantly worried. Owning your thoughts and emotions puts you on track to living your best life. When you are peaceful and content, then people and situations will respond to your happy state of being. As you begin to take control over your emotional state, you create the life you want.

This is where you need to catch yourself from going into over-thinking. You know the thoughts but how, what, where and when start to creep in. This is what keeps you in a perpetual loop of "Yes, I'm happy but..."

When you are going into the overthinking mode, then you are still in a state of worry and lack of trust within yourself. This is where my question, *how well do you really know yourself?*, comes in. This is your opportunity to own exactly where your thoughts go. It is a practice to shift how you think.

How would it feel to always be empowered? No matter what may be going on in your life, you can choose how you feel at any given moment.

Knowing yourself and that your peace is a priority allows you to be emotionally neutral, which allows for clarity and how to handle the speed bumps of life. As most people do, you may tend to cycle back around to old thought processes. Always ask yourself: *what is it I am meant to learn?* Then release it.

Your mind is the storehouse for absolutely everything you have experienced in life, which has created your behavior patterns. So yes, it is wise to visit those aspects of yourself that you have been afraid to face. It doesn't have to be hard to unlock old patterns, but when you do, life becomes magical. Owning your emotional well-being is what sets the stage for bigger and better things.

Choose Your Empowered Life

- Starting your day in gratitude puts you in a happy state.
- Notice the beauty around you.
- Meditate.
- Eat clean healthy food.
- Exercise, not just your body but your mind, too.
- Be loving.
- Heal your shadow aspects.
- Show up in your power.
- Allow life to happen for you.
- Be peaceful and content.

It is liberating to be at peace! You will begin to notice you have more energy to handle your day-to-day tasks with ease, allowing for more creative ideas to flow. This could simply be *aha* moments of how you once were.

Coming into a new version of yourself is exciting. Suddenly everything changes. Having a new perspective, you then set the tone of how you would like to create your life. What is it that you really want to do, but haven't? You will begin to feel that nothing is impossible.

With this level of clarity, it becomes easier to focus on what your next steps will be. Have you wanted to change careers, start your own company, or have more time and freedom to travel? Whatever it may be, you are on the right track to go after your heart's desires. Now you will notice the magic in what comes your way.

You get to create and control your empowered life! Sounds exciting, right!? This is when you push all fear aside. At the end of the day, it does not matter what anyone thinks. This is your personal journey. Allow your excellence to shine and dare to jump into the life you wish you always had.

Now you will be open to opportunities that were not there

before. When you are living your best life, you will become a beacon of light and the right people and situations will appear as if by magic.

What does that look like to you?

It may be better relationships, or a more fulfilling career. Set your intentions from this elevated happy way of being and you will see the beauty in everything. Giving you the chance to live into this free-flowing energy will allow for true contentment.

Dare to Dream!

When was the last time you allowed yourself to daydream? You are safe to go after what you want! Take a moment and think about all the things you would like to experience. This process should feel exciting.

Notice how your body also responds along with your thoughts. Allow yourself to feel like a child. You know how children are, when they want something, they expect it. They never think of any reason why they can't have it. So dream like a child, and put your thoughts into motion toward what it is you would like.

That's it! Stay positive, and allow yourself to come into vibrational alignment with your own creation. Take note of how your intuition becomes stronger, and you will be able to navigate life accordingly.

Remember you first, then you will see your life fall into place. When you hold your personal power higher, then others will communicate from a level of respect, giving you a sense of happiness that everyone around you will benefit from.

Life can be happy and abundant if you allow it. Guard your peace so your happiness becomes a blessing for others.

Go live and create by being happy. Allow yourself to be delighted by all the synchronicities that will come your way.

Always taking a bird's eye view will show you what is important to you. Never sweating the small stuff. Coming from this higher perspective you will notice what no longer deserves your attention.

Have fun in all that you do. Beam your soul light and enjoy every step you take. Everything is always in divine timing so trust the process.

Live!

Be Happy!

Enjoy Your Empowered Life!

Chapter Eight

Unlock Your Communication Potential
By Avarel Smith

Avarel M. Smith is a Certified Dating and Relationship Coach and former Matchmaker. So naturally, single women turn to her for help breaking their toxic dating cycles and recognizing their true worth, so they can create the love life they desire and deserve.

As Founder and CEO of Seeking Synergy, she is passionate about empowering and educating women on becoming the best versions of themselves, while living unapologetically and authentically.

Relationships and finances go hand in hand. So, she is proud to be a licensed Insurance Agent, helping individuals protect their families, while building generational wealth.

Avarel takes a holistic approach to coaching. She nurtures her client's journey of self-discovery and making the transformative steps towards their emotional, physical, personal, financial and spiritual growth.

Are you having trust issues, lack of communication or the inability to resolve conflict? Avarel's ultimate course will transform your relationship and your life.

www.seekingsynergyforlife.com/building-trust-to-foster-a-lasting-connection.

www.linkedin.com/in/avarelsmith

www.instagram.com/seeking_synergyforlife

www.facebook.com/SeekingSynergy

www.tiktok.com/@seeking_synergy

www.seekingsynergyforlife.com

Unlock Your Communication Potential

By Avarel Smith

Having worked with countless women who struggle with various aspects of their relationships, I have observed one particular topic that consistently stands out as a major concern for most women: Communication.

Communication is an essential component of any relationship, yet it is often the source of misunderstandings, conflicts, and even breakups.

Relationships are an integral part of our lives, whether they are with our partner, family or friends. They can bring immense joy and support, but can also cause stress and conflict.

As women, we often carry the weight of nurturing and maintaining these relationships, which can be challenging and exhausting.

I'll dive into the topic of communication in relationships and provide practical guidance to help enhance your skills. We'll explore different styles, look at barriers that often prevent effective communication, and discover strategies to overcome these barriers and improve the way you communicate with others.

Mastering the art of communication is crucial for building and maintaining healthy relationships. It doesn't matter if you're in a committed relationship, just starting out, or looking to improve how you converse with family members or friends. These tips will be invaluable in helping you achieve your relationship goals.

Whether you are looking to resolve conflicts, express your needs and desires, or simply connect with your partner on a deeper level, this chapter will also provide you with the tools and knowledge to communicate effectively and build trust to create stronger, more fulfilling relationships.

Living a Life of Purpose

Living your best life means different things to different people, but at its core, it's about creating a life that aligns with your values, passions, and goals. It's about prioritizing your well-being, pursuing personal growth, and finding joy and fulfillment in your everyday experiences.

It's also about taking control of your life and making intentional choices that lead to a sense of purpose and happiness. While this may sound like a lofty concept, it applies to you in practical ways.

Improving your communication skills is one way to live your best life. It has numerous benefits, both personal and professional.

Some Are:

1. Better expressing your thoughts and feelings: It empowers you to articulate your thoughts and emotions in a clear, concise, and respectful manner. Expressing your needs, desires, and boundaries leads to more fulfilling relationships with those around you.
2. Resolving conflicts: This lets you express your concerns and perspectives in a constructive way. Learning to listen actively, empathize with others, and find common ground leads to more harmonious relationships.
3. Building trust: It allows you to connect on a deeper and more meaningful level. By expressing your vulnerabilities, you foster a sense of trust, respect, and intimacy in your relationships.

These skills ultimately enhance your overall well-being. You'll feel more confident and empowered to make important decisions and take control of your life.

Become a Captain Communicator

Communication is the glue that holds any relationship together.

However, I think it's fair to say that all of us have had real-life run-ins with a communication problem. After all, we weren't taught how to be good communicators, right?

We all communicate in different ways and on different levels. Yet, lack of communication in any relationship wreaks havoc for everyone.

 People hear your words, but they feel your attitude.

— John C. Maxwell

Here Are Key Ways to Master the Art of Communication:

1. Acknowledge that a problem exists. Then identify the source.
2. Process your feelings. Take time to fully understand all the emotions you're feeling.
3. Pay attention to your tone of voice, body language and attitude.
4. Be willing to listen for understanding. Talk less, listen more. Communication without comprehension is futile.
5. Be open to the other person's perspective. It's NOT all about you.
6. Discuss your feelings. Use "I" statements. *"I feel hurt when you raise your voice"* rather than *"You always shout at me."*
7. Compromise. Meet in the middle.

It's also crucial to be mindful of these communication styles and how they can affect your relationships.

1. **Assertive Communication** — Direct but compassionate and non-threatening. Allows the other person to express him/herself without fear of being judged or criticized.
2. **Aggressive Communication** — Hostile, intimidating, or threatening. Verbal and nonverbal communication, such as raising your voice, making threats, or using physical force.
3. **Passive Communication** — Avoids conflict. However, you don't challenge the other person or stand up for yourself.
4. **Passive Aggressive Communication** — Indirect, hostile and manipulative. Making subtle hints or hurtful comments, while avoiding direct confrontation.

Credibility Cultivates Closeness

Building trust in your relationship is also an essential principle of living your best life and a key component of the communication process. Trust is the foundation of all healthy relationships, built through consistent communication and follow-through.

When you establish trust, you create an environment of safety and mutual respect, which can enhance your overall well-being.

My clients use this exercise to cultivate trust with their partner.

Hold a *"Trust Chat"*

Ask each other tough questions like:

1. What do trust and commitment mean to you?

2. What kind of expectations do you have for sexual and emotional monogamy or fidelity?
3. What expectations do you have regarding money, time together, and children/family?

This conversation will open up a whole new level of intimacy, give you a sense of how much you trust one another, and whether you view trust and commitment in the same way.

Awaken The Conflict Conqueror Within You

Resolving conflict constructively is another crucial practice in living your best life. Conflict is a natural part of any relationship, so it's important to learn how to manage it productively.

The key is to approach conflict with an open mind, listen actively, and communicate clearly and respectfully. By doing so, you find solutions that work for everyone involved and avoid resentment and bitterness.

Unresolved conflict can cause anxiety and depression, which can have a serious impact on your mental health.

This stress can also lead to ailments such as headaches, digestive problems and high blood pressure.

Here Are 4 Strategic Ways to Resolve Conflict Constructively:

1. **Timing is everything** — The best time to resolve conflict is right away. Addressing issues quickly avoids escalation. However, if needed, discuss a convenient time to talk about it. You may need to calm down before having a conversation. Also, validate the person's feelings, rather than dismiss them.
2. **Don't kitchen sink** — Women are more likely to engage in kitchen sinking. It's taking everything you can

think of that has annoyed you over the past week, month or even year and throwing it at the other person. Instead, focus on the current issue at hand.

3. **Lose the absolutes. Refrain from ultimatums** — Don't use "never" and "always." No one is always something or never anything. Avoid making threats, demands or stipulations such as "If you don't do ABC, I'll do XYZ."

4. **Apologize** — "I am sorry" are three powerful words and people just don't say them often enough. Saying sorry shows a willingness to take responsibility for your actions and that you're open to making amends.

Roadblocks to Remove

As women, we face a range of obstacles daily. Some are societal expectations, self-sabotaging beliefs, relationship challenges and dealing with setbacks.

There's a lot of negative self-talk, perfectionism, and imposter syndrome, which undermines your self-confidence and prevents you from pursuing your goals and dreams.

To overcome self-sabotaging beliefs, practice self-compassion, challenge negative thoughts, and focus on your strengths and accomplishments.

Prioritize your own values and needs in relationships. Communicate them assertively and set boundaries early with your partner and others.

Reframe your mindset and view setbacks as opportunities for growth and learning. Set realistic goals and break them down into small, achievable steps.

Practice self-care, self-love and treat yourself with kindness. Recognize that making mistakes is a natural part of the learning process, so give yourself grace. And remember, self-love is the key to finding true love.

Strengthen your mindset through positive daily affirmations. Write them down and say them out loud every day. You'll be amazed at how much you start to believe them.

Reach out to mentors or trusted family and friends who can provide guidance and support.

Communicate, Captivate and Celebrate your Existence

The art of communication is not something that can be mastered overnight. It requires patience, practice, and self-reflection.

Living your best life is not about attaining perfection or conforming to societal expectations. It's about embracing your unique journey, accepting the power of your voice, and fostering authentic connections with yourself and others.

Acknowledge that conflicts are opportunities for growth and transformation, and that effective communication can bridge gaps and bring you closer to your goals.

So approach communication with intention, empathy, and a commitment to understanding. By doing so, you empower yourself to live your best life, embracing the joy, fulfillment, and authenticity that await you as a woman.

Chapter Nine

Spirituali-Tea' is My Priori-Tea for Eterni-Tea

By Anna Lugo

Anna Lugo is the Owner of Pure Tea Love & Pure CBD Love. She launched her first business 'Pure CBD Love on 11/11/2020 during COVID. She launched Pure Tea Love on 2/22/22. Anna is a retired I.T. professional, a single mother, and Entrepreneur and a woman after God's Heart. She also host a show on Everyday Woman TV called **We Have A Tea For That... Positivi-Tea!** Her goal is to Inspire at least One Person A Day if not More.

www.linkedin.com/in/AnnALugo
www.instagram.com/Alohalugo
www.facebook.com/AnnaBarbozaLugo
www.puretealove.com

Spirituali-Tea' is My Priori-Tea for Eterni-Tea

By Anna Lugo

Living Your Best Life to Me is Putting God First!...
My Spirituali-Tea' is My Priori-Tea, for Eterni-Tea.
I Always Say "I'm Too Blessed To Be Stressed."

To Me Living My Best Life Begins with my daily walk with God. I'm a Prayer Warrior and my Spirituali-Tea is my Priority for Eternal-Tea. My prayer life is Important. It's important to Me, it's who I Am, it's what I Am. It's my honor to be a prayer warrior!

There are so many Opportuni-Teas and the Possibili-Teas are endless when it comes to living a life of Faith. I love being "In service" to others and to myself. I take this Responsibili-Tea seriously. Holding myself to a higher degree and level of Integri-Tea, and Authenticity (Authentici-Tea). I love that my Generosi-Tea allows me to bless others through a Varie-Teas of Chari-Tea's. I support Inclusion, Diversi-Tea and Equali-Tea. I appreciate transparency and Sinceri-Tea, I'm thankful and blessed to live in Prosperi-Tea and am truly grateful to those who stood behind me with great Loyal-Tea.

I work hard to surround myself with like minded individuals. Where Tranquili-Tea and Sereni-Tea thrive.

A Communi-Tea of Leaders such as you and Me to recognize we get to Live with purpose, and Longivi-Tea. When we tap into our Feminin-Tea, or Masculinity or sensuality we own our true self-worth. When we Love ourselves and watch what we are feeding our minds, our creative juices begin flowing. We can achieve greatness. It's up to Us to recognize & discover that with God All Things Are Possible and we gain a Power like no other. Sometimes our Anxiety and our Curiosi-Tea's can get the best of us but we have to push forward with full Vitali-Tea. Of course, it takes Clari-Tea and constant Communication with the Man upstairs. Victory, Vitali-Tea, and Visibility is what is around the next corner. We can always find an encouraging word, an Inspiring word, a hopeful word and stand strong in A Faith that surpasses understanding.

I know that if I put God First in Everything I do, His hand will be in Everything I do. My faith is strong because at a very young age my Mother taught me to pray before I even understood what prayer was. I learned over the years that prayer is a conversation between You & God. I talk to and I Trust Him to ordain my every step every single day. My first thought of the day is one of Thanks!

I learned to be clear and specific for what is behind my "I Am" is ALL POWERFUL. It takes work to be intentional with your I AM'.... What's Behind Your *I Am?*

> *I Am A Visionary, I Am Enough, I Am Worthy of*
> *Love, I am Grateful, I Am Unique, I am Loving, I*
> *Am A Doer, I Am Blessed, I am Light, I am*
> *Faithful, I am Phenomenal, I am Respected, I am*
> *an Independent Woman, I am Passionate, I am a*
> *Champion, I Am God's Masterpiece. I Am*
> *Special. I am a Child of God. I Am Thankful. I*
> *Am Blessed. What are you saying? Always*
> *remember What you put behind your I AM*
> *defines YOU.*

Another daily task/habit I do Everyday, is to Dream, Declare, and Deliver three things every single day. Big or Small, it does not matter. Declare them by 9am and clear them by 9pm. I learned that you will either keep your word with yourself or you won't. This is really a test of Integrity.

I have been happily married and happily divorced. I've also had my share of heartache and loss. The beautiful irony is, when the thing that threatens to destroy you the most is the only thing that makes you stronger, it sets you Free. Only after I completely Let Go and Let God did I realize my worth. I've been abused, misused, disrespected, neglected, and verbally, mentally, and physically beaten down.

However, I refused to stay down. The saying get knocked down 7 times get up 8 has always been a saying in my life.

But after attending an Intellectual Leadership Training course 14 years ago, I discovered that EVERYTHING in LIFE is A CHOICE. I went through a TRANSFORMATIONAL experience where I had to peel the Onion to get to the Core of my being. Where I discovered my beliefs and limited beliefs. Where I finally discovered and found myself. Where I had an opportunity to face myself and get to the core Of my Soul.

Where I learned to have breakthrough after breakthrough to get to the core of a much needed experience where I learned to be vulnerable with my heart ripped wide open to discover who I was. Doing the required work to be Raw, to be Transparent, to be intentional. I learned to find my voice and set clear and healthy boundaries. I learned what I wanted to be, how I wanted to showed up vs. How I was Showing up. I learned to Let Go and Let God. I AM in Awe of my bodies Abili-Tea to heal. When You learn to say no to trauma and drama you set yourself free. I'm happy I was able to transform and mature at the young age of 50 where I finally got my Voice, and Believe me now that I have it I will use it to speak and inspire words of encouragement and set healthy boundaries. You are not going to master the BEST of your Life in one day you have to master today and do that Everyday day after day.

I learned that when you create a habit for 100 days it becomes a habit for life. I learned to be Grateful for my every blessing in life. I like to do an exercise where I write down 3 to 5 things in my gratitude journal that I am grateful for. Then, I like to take it a step further and think of 3 reasons why you are thankful for each item. You will soon notice that you are abundantly blessed and your gratitude will soar. Also be conscious of the ships in your life. Companionship, Friendships, Relationships, Mentorships, Entrepreneurship, and Fellowships, if they are not taking you anywhere it is best to abandon ship. As you move through this Life stay in gratitude. Be grateful for the magical experiences that leave you in AWE. Be prepared for shifts, shakes, twists, turns, and know they are sometimes necessary in order to grow, glow, learn and evolve into the Best version of yourself. Know that SHIFT Happens!! Be ready to Love and be Loved to accept and be accepted. Lead by example, be a role model and display an attitude of gratitude and watch your life produce more blessings to cherish a lifetime. This life is Not a dress Rehearsal.

> *In Closing A Prayer for You!*
> *I pray for you my sweet friends as I pray for myself. I*
> *pray for Life to be kind to you. For the right people*
> *to come into your path and raise you up and not*
> *tear you down. I pray you stay committed to your*
> *dreams and heart's desires. I pray that you know*
> *your worth and that words of love reach you when*
> *you need it most. I pray that you set healthy*
> *routines and habits that help you elevate into your*
> *highest potential. May all your sorrows stay at bay*
> *and hugs reach you. I pray you recognize the many*
> *blessings seen and unseen, I pray that you feel*
> *deeply Blessed for this journey we call LIFE.*
> *I Pray You Keep Living Your Best Life... Amen*

Chapter Ten

Living Ambitiously
By Anjené Abston

Anjené Abston is a Life Coach specializing in supporting busy people achieve their life ambitions.

An accomplished professional with 16+ years of business experience, Anjené's expertise is operational excellence and risk management. She has traveled to 40+ countries and is a lifelong learner.

By the age of 30, Anjené was promoted to Vice President and knows finding balance while climbing the corporate ladder can be exhausting. Becoming an executive at a young age, she learned the importance of setting boundaries, having non-career goals and maintaining a social life.

Anjené became a coach to support those who struggle to "have it all" and help them avoid pitfalls. Anjené focuses on prioritization, goal execution, professional development and travel.

Anjené holds an M.S. from Northwestern University (Information Systems Security), a B.S. from Miami University, Ohio (Marketing / Sociology), attended a Wharton School of Business Executive Development program plus earned 7 professional certifications.

www.linkedin.com/company/livingambitiously
www.instagram.com/living_ambitiously
www.facebook.com/livingambitiouslycoach
https://imlivingambitiously.com

Living Ambitiously

By Anjené Abston

I believe living one's best life is subjective. It means something completely different from one person to the next. How you live your life is very personal. Which is why for the everyday woman, it's important to be intentional about how life is structured for it to be the best possible version she desires. In this chapter, I will walk you through ways to accomplish this.

No matter what the circumstances of one's life, I would argue we all want to be healthy, to give / receive love, and enjoy our lives. For me, those are fundamental truths. With this as the baseline, I think we can have our most desirable life.

Some may have more obstacles than others. Some must make the best out of a challenging situation. Sometimes it's about being in survival mode before you get to be in a place of mental and/or physical freedom. Ultimately how we live our life is a choice. We make choices every day, whether we realize it or not. Sometimes we do things out of habit, sometimes it's deliberate. I have found planning drives you to having the life you want.

Ever since I was a young adult, I've looked for ways to have the best life possible. I have done quite a bit of soul searching and being self-aware of what makes me happy and what does not. What situations are healthy for me to be in, and which ones are not beneficial at all. Having that background knowledge helps me to navigate the type of life I want to have. I look for what brings me joy. While it may be completely impossible to avoid every adverse circumstance, knowing what I can control allows me to steer down the right path.

I have witnessed many people, both personally and professionally, who have not lived joyful lives. For whatever reason, they sacrifice their long-term happiness. It's one thing if you are sucking up something for a defined time frame to achieve a goal but when there's no end-date, it's quite different. It holds a distinct energy which can impact various parts of one's life. This is why I think it's vital to incorporate intention, self-reflection, and a supportive network into your life.

An example of this is when I decided to pursue my master's degree. Before I even finished my bachelor's degree, I knew I would one day get my 2nd degree. It was just the "when" in question and in some instances, the "what." After more than a decade of deliberating on what type of program (online), the time commitment I could feel comfortable with (1 course per quarter) and the subject matter (Information Systems Security), I finally went back to school while working. To say it was challenging would be an understatement, but I believe I chose wisely. Even though at times when working on an assignment I would feel like I was literally paying to torture myself, I was overall happy with my decision. During the 3 years I was in my program, I switched jobs, went on 2 amazing vacations, and found time to have enough social and family interactions to not feel like I completely disappeared. Did I miss out on some stuff? Yes, of course! But everything has an opportunity cost.

I have a saying, "you can do anything, but you can't do everything." It's something I've used many times over the years. I've tried to do "everything" all at once before and it can be disastrous, unless you either don't need to sleep or have a team of people who are there to handle all the nuanced parts of life. There's a time and place for all the things we want to do. And I fully believe you should do what you want but is the timing the most appropriate or realistic? If you have 10 things going on simultaneously, is it a good idea to add an 11th item? To evaluate, ask yourself the following:

- What's the time commitment in terms of frequency and term? (once / week over 2 years)
- How will this impact the other areas of your life? (romance, children, social)

- What value are you going to get out of this additional commitment? (new skill, business development, philanthropic goals)

If the answers to these questions are all positive, then perhaps it makes sense to move forward with the commitment. If they aren't, it may need a discussion about when, if ever, is the best time to pursue the item. It really comes down to self-negotiating what your priorities are. Everything cannot be the #1 priority.

For me, living my best life means Living Ambitiously. That's exactly why it's the name of my business. It's a daily reminder of the type of life I want to live and help others to achieve. I know living a fulfilling and meaningful life is a journey. You don't simply get to your best life and then chill. It's a constant work in progress because the ideal may change over time. On a macro level, it's because society is constantly in fluctuation which could have direct and/or indirect impacts on how you live your life. On a micro level, it's due to our own mental growth and daily personal experiences. What you wanted as your best life in your 20s is likely different than what you want in your 40s. Knowing this will help prepare for change as those shifts happen.

It's important to set up strategies and routines to ensure you live your life the way you want at any given point in time. Take time to check in with yourself, at minimum once a year, and with those whom your life directly impacts on a personal level as to what changes are occurring. One way of doing this is to make 1-, 5- and 10-year plans which will help to set the tone of where you want to go and know what actions will need to be taken to get there. It will also give you the ability to have regular insight into where your priorities are. If you are focusing your time and attention on an area which isn't going to get you to your goal, you can evaluate if you want to continue down that path.

Life is fluid. No two days are the same. Since your desires this year could be completely different than next, completing the Wheel of Life exercise is another great way to course correct. It's a tool I offer my clients and have found to be eye-opening. It has repeatedly helped me evaluate where I currently stand and where to adjust. It allows you to visually see what you're focused on and what you need to pay attention to.

An in-the-moment method to use is to take stock of instances when you're having a lot of doubt, feeling challenged, and struggling. Ask yourself questions about what's going on internally.

- This doesn't feel good, but what's the reason I'm being triggered by this feeling?
- Are my feelings / instincts saying something needs to change?
- Do I need to take a day (or 7) to sit with this and figure out what's going on?

My favorite method is traveling. I personally love an international trip to explore someplace new. But this works even with a weekend getaway or crashing at a friend's home for a night to regenerate and clear your mind. I find traveling can be such a healing experience. Picking the right type of travel will energize you even more. Sometimes I need to just sit at a beach. Or perhaps what I need is to do a bit of trekking around to explore nature. And other times it's just people watching at a café on a Parisian street. Each trip has a different feel but can allow a mental reset and see what may not be obvious when you're in your daily routine.

Unfortunately, life isn't always sunny and joyful. However, for most life events, there are mitigating factors which can be put into place to help alleviate disruptive conditions. I don't know if it's the risk management professional in me, but I'm frequently thinking of ways to make things better in case something happens. I'm all about the convenience in life and when it's interrupted, it throws many things out of whack. And I've learned I'm not too fond of when this occurs. So now I proactively look for ways to reduce those chances.

It's not uncommon to experience anxiety, regret, or self-doubt throughout some point in time. The skill to learn is to not sit in negativity. Life isn't going to stop because you're having a bad day, month, or year. You must develop the courage to move forward and keep striving to have the life you want. There will be setbacks. We just can't control everything. If you're an over-analyzing thinker like me, you must learn to get out of your own head to know when you can't control something and maybe sometimes when you just shouldn't. Scary, right? It doesn't have to be, if you mentally prepare for when things go wrong and proactively put the right support in place.

Ultimately, I believe prioritization, healthy relationships, fortitude, and well-established boundaries are key to a balanced and gratifying life.

Time to check in... do you feel like you are not currently living your best life? If that's the case, take action now! Incremental increases go a long way. You don't have to do a complete overhaul of your life. Find 3-5 things you can do to make things a bit better. Rinse and repeat until you become more satisfied with how your life is set up. We all deserve to be happy and feel like the life we're living is a good one.

If you are struggling or feel overwhelmed with doing this alone, find those in your network who can support you through this. I'm also a resource you can tap into.

I wish everyone reading this book an amazing, healthy, and ambitious life!

Chapter Eleven

Managing Through Struggles into Thriving
By Denise Hansard

Denise Hansard, Life Architect, Intuitive & Motivational Speaker Author of *Suffering In Comfort* (Available on Amazon)

As a transformational Life Coach, Denise uses her intuition and strategic mind to work with clients on a journey for claiming their worth & love of self above all else in their life to create everything else in their life.

She works with successful women & men who are looking for

that next step in their life ... the second half of their career and/or life finding fulfillment, satisfaction, and a sense of purpose.

With a Masters in Counseling, a Certification in Life Coaching and 20 years in the corporate world (Certified Pricing Professional), she's an expert in transformation and change.

www.linkedin.com/in/denisehansard

www.instagram.com/denisehansardcoach

www.facebook.com/Coaching2Dream?ref=bookmarks

www.denisehansard.com

www.my.timetrade.com/book/9KPX2

www.tiktok.com/@seeking_synergy

Managing Through Struggles into Thriving

By Denise Hansard

As a life architect, I get to walk alongside people as they face some of the most difficult moments of their lives. The reason I feel equipped to do that is because I have faced some of the darkest moments human beings can experience. Way more than I've wanted. Having been able to walk through those dark nights, as I have, has helped me to choose to live my best life even in the dark moments. That is what I want to share with you today.

After being with my person for eight and a half years, he decided to end his life. He was the one who helped to pull curiosity out of me, and when he felt he could no longer face his struggles and committed suicide, I felt desperate and alone. I knew that I could choose the same option he had. The aspirin and tequila were keeping me company one night when I heard an inner voice ask me one of those curiosity-based questions, "What would this do to your family?"

As that question sank in fully - to the deepest darkest part of my soul, I knew I couldn't follow through with my plans. But that wasn't the end of my season of struggle. In an attempt to make myself invisible so that I could hide myself away, I gained 20 pounds. Not a great look on a petite woman barely reaching 5'2" without teased hair. You see, I didn't want anyone to notice me, talk to me, or ask me any important questions.

It took me around 10 years of living this way, as if I was my own shadow, before I finally let those healing, curious questions back into my life. The first one that popped into my head when I was willing to listen was *"Am I living the kind of life that I want?"*

Once I was finally honest with myself, I realized I was tired of living that way and I mentally flipped the switch. I worked hard to restore not just my body, but also my spirit. And I worked to find myself, my light, in the midst of that darkness.

After that journey, I realized I was stronger than before. My path out of the unknown depths of despair into the light inspired the life I now live and choose every day. My personal experience of knowing what life can be like on the other side is one of the biggest reasons I love what I do. Because no matter what you're going through in life— no matter where you've been — there's always a way to embrace the path that helps you shine your light into the world both, personally and professionally.

This transformative journey not only brought me out of the shadows but also propelled me towards living my best life. A life where I grew stronger through every challenge placed before me, and there have been many.

Many years after my journey and transformation, I was given the opportunity to embrace another dark night.

In the corporate world, I found myself dissatisfied, moving from one company to another, feeling disconnected from a life I truly loved. Then, the universe presented me with a challenge—a test of how well I had learned to live my best life.

The company I was in began facing financial difficulties, resulting in numerous layoffs across departments. I knew my turn was approaching as my boss scheduled a one-on-one meeting with me late in the afternoon. The moment arrived, and as he uttered the words, "I have to let you and your whole team go," a wave of emotions washed over me. Yet, in that very moment, I embraced the challenge and chose to live my best life.

With tears welling in my eyes, I mustered the courage to say, "Thank you. This is a blessing in disguise." My boss was taken aback, hastily directing me to HR.

Surprisingly, this dark night moment passed with greater ease than I had anticipated. It dawned on me that my previous tendencies to hide and fall into despair were no longer viable options. I had evolved beyond that. I celebrated this personal growth. By listening to my inner voice of knowing, I embarked on the path I tread today working as a life coach, transforming lives.

Living my best life in every dark night moment became a deliberate choice, a conscious commitment to embracing joy, fulfillment, and authenticity. I learned to align my actions with my values, to pursue meaningful relationships, and to nurture my passions. Each day became an opportunity to make a positive difference in the lives of others and to contribute to a more compassionate and empathetic world.

My personal experiences serve as a constant reminder of the resilience and strength that lie within us all. They fuel my dedication to helping individuals overcome their own challenges and discover their own unique paths towards a life that radiates light and purpose.

Through the darkness of those experiences I've faced, I found the key to living my best life, and now it is my greatest privilege to guide others towards embracing their own journeys of self-discovery, growth, and empowerment.

When faced with the type of challenges described, embarking on a transformative journey of healing and personal growth requires a deeper exploration. Here are three profound steps that women can take to navigate this path:

1. **Embrace the Journey:** Embracing change and healing is like embarking on an exciting adventure. Remember that it takes time and it's okay to enjoy the twists and turns along the way. Allow yourself to feel the emotions and give yourself permission to grow at your own pace.

2. **Rediscover Your Beautiful Self:** Take this opportunity to reconnect with the marvelous person you are today, knowing your journey is beginning and you want more. Engage in self-reflection with a sprinkle of curiosity and delve into what truly brings you joy and fulfillment. Set intentions that align with your values and desires and take small steps towards personal growth and empowerment. Celebrate your authenticity

as it shines brightly through the changes you've experienced.

3. **Give Back and Find Meaning:** Finding meaning and purpose can be a powerful part of managing through struggles to live your best life. Consider ways to give back and make a positive impact in your community or in causes close to your heart. Whether it's volunteering, supporting others facing similar challenges, or using your own unique experiences to raise awareness and ignite a fire for change, you'll find a sense of fulfillment in uplifting others. Your light will illuminate the path for both you and those around you.

One more story for you ...

Another dark night was losing my mom after moving in to take care of her in the last months of her life. It was the best of times and the worst of times, as they say. However, the true challenge began after her passing — the journey of healing.

Through my grief, I found solace in knowing that my mom's spirit still lingered with me. It was in this realization of the precious gifts — gifts of love, compassion, and patience. Patience became my companion as I navigated through the feelings of inadequacy, questioning whether I had been enough for her and for myself. It was also patience that carried me through moments of self-doubt regarding my ability to serve my clients and nurture my business. Yet, amidst it all, time became my ally, unveiling the truth that I was more than enough —more than my mother could have ever imagined, and more than I could have ever fathomed.

To live your best life, embrace the dark nights that come. Here is where the valuable lessons lie along with profound growth. Embrace your unique gifts and strengths, allowing them to guide you through the journey. However, remember that strength also lies in accepting support from others. Sometimes, leaning on the kindness and assistance of those around us is an act of courage. As fear may emerge, view it as a dance partner—a companion that, when embraced, can lead to beautiful transformations and breakthroughs.

Amidst the challenges, listen closely to the whispers of love and guidance that reside within. Embrace the darkness, dance with your fears, and trust your journey will unfold in ways that exceed your wildest dreams.

If you find yourself seeking guidance and support, reach out. Together, we can navigate the complexities of life while embarking on a transformative journey filled with joy, strength, and the opportunity to radiate your beautiful light into the world.

Chapter Twelve

Recognize, Protect, Focus and Repeat!
by Becky McCrea

Becky McCrea is a multi-talented business owner, technologist, children's book author, and advocate for women in IT. With a track record of success, she has created award-winning software for the State of Iowa, launched a farmer-connecting mobile app, and delivers custom Salesforce solutions with her team at AppLifts.

As a visionary entrepreneur and tech trailblazer, Becky's innovative ideas and commitment to excellence have left a profound impact on the industry, inspiring countless aspiring entrepreneurs. She's driven by empowering others and has a special mission to promote self-awareness and overcome self-doubt through her children's book and workbooks.

Becky resides in Iowa with her husband and two active children, sharing joyful family moments through soccer and travel.

www.linkedin.com/in/beckymccrea
www.instagram.com/growfromglow
www.facebook.com/growfromglow
www.growfromglow.com

Recognize, Protect, Focus and Repeat!

by Becky McCrea

Living your best life means different things to different people, but it generally involves feeling fulfilled, happy, and content with your life. If you feel like you're already living your best life, it's likely because you're doing things that align with your values and bring you joy and satisfaction. If you're not living your best life, it's important to take steps to make positive changes each day. Reading this book and taking inspiration from each of the chapters is a great way to instill positive changes in your life and remind you that you deserve the life of your dreams!

To live your best life, you must first identify what you want out of life. This requires introspection and self-reflection. You need to understand what motivates you, what you value, and what makes you happy. Once you have a clear understanding of these things, you can start to create a plan for how you will achieve them. It's okay not to have all the answers immediately. The unknown of what you want may cause frustration, anxiety, and a lack of fulfillment. However, the best part of the journey to life fulfillment is realizing you don't have to have all the answers.

If you feel like living your best life is out of reach, consider these helpful tips to help you regain momentum, find the answers to what makes you happy, and get back on track:

1. **Identify Your Core Values.** Reflect on the principles that guide your decisions and actions. When you start thinking about why you made a particular decision or why you performed an action, you will start learning about what makes you tick. Did you like the outcomes? If not, adjust and move on. Your core values

are the foundation of your authentic self, and aligning with them will lead to a more fulfilling life.

2. **Explore Your Passions.** Engage in activities that genuinely interest you. Whether it's trying a new hobby, taking a class, or volunteering for a cause, exploring different experiences can help you uncover what brings you joy and fulfillment. Doing more of what makes you happy will ultimately lead to higher life satisfaction.

3. **Journal Regularly.** Maintain a journal to record your thoughts, reflections, and progress. Writing can help you gain clarity and insights into your true desires and aspirations. If you don't feel comfortable or are not sure what to write about, a guided journal may be helpful.

Identifying what you want and living your best life is a voyage that requires patience, self-compassion, and courage. Remember that self-discovery is an ongoing process, and it's normal to encounter challenges along the way. By engaging in self-reflection and embracing new experiences, you can gradually uncover your passions, values, and aspirations, leading you toward a more fulfilling and authentic life.

Once you identify what you want out of life, you can establish goals that genuinely support your journey toward living your best life and experiencing true fulfillment. These goals will provide you with direction, purpose, and a sense of accomplishment as you progress on the path of personal growth and happiness. There are many ways to track goals and I encourage you to reflect on how you feel each time your goal is achieved. If you are feeling good, accomplished, and satisfied, then you know you are on the right track. If you don't feel excited about your achievements, it may be time to re-evaluate and reset your goals to better align with your new perspective.

Pursuing a fulfilled life is about finding meaning, joy, and satisfaction in our existence. It goes beyond momentary happiness and encompasses a deeper connection with ourselves, others, and the world around us. When we prioritize fulfillment, we unlock the potential for a life of purpose, growth, and profound well-being.

While living your best life is possible, most people don't achieve it. Here are some reasons why:

1. **Fear of failure.** Many people are afraid to pursue their dreams because they are afraid of failing. They may worry about what others will think if they don't succeed, or fear that they won't be able to support themselves financially. This fear can be paralyzing, preventing them from taking risks and pursuing their passions, therefore, leading to going through the motions day in and day out and living a lackluster life.

2. **Lack of direction.** Some people simply don't know what they want out of life. They may feel lost or unsure of what their values and goals are, making it difficult to create a plan for living their best life. They also don't take the steps to seek clarity or find their passions by trying new things.

3. **Lack of motivation.** Even those who know what they want may lack the motivation to take action. It can be easy to get stuck in a rut, feeling unmotivated and uninspired to make changes in your life. Not living your best life is the easy path because you don't have to make changes; you get to live in your comfort zone.

4. **External pressures.** Many people feel pressure from external sources, such as society, friends, or family, to conform to certain expectations. They may feel like they have to pursue a certain career or have a certain lifestyle to make other people happy. People pleasing is a real pandemic and the sooner you realize you get to make choices that benefit you, the faster you will be on your way to happiness.

It's important to remember that living your best life doesn't mean everything is perfect. Everyone faces challenges and setbacks, but how you respond to those challenges can make a big difference. If you're able to stay positive and resilient in the face of adversity, you're more likely to feel fulfilled and happy. A lot of people focus on the struggle and like Carl Jung profoundly said, 'What you resist persists.'

A simple way to get back on track is to use my **Recognize, Protect, and Focus Method**:

Recognize your unhappiness and discontent.

Embrace and acknowledge your feelings and then let them go. Progress is not made by choosing to continue to feel discontent with your life, instead take action by trying to do one small thing that brings you joy. It can be very rewarding to journal how you're feeling, what happened, and how you are going to choose to react to similar situations in the future. Identify your specific triggers and stressors and work to avoid those in the future. If you can identify the root causes of dissatisfaction, it makes it easier to recognize certain patterns in life that you might want to change for the better.

Protect your peace.

This step is huge. It is very important to establish healthy boundaries in your life. This may cause stress to other people and your relationships with them, but your peace is vital to living a fulfilled life. This may also require you to recognize and set limits on negative influences such as social media. Learning to say no to draining commitments and embracing self-care practices are both healthy for your wellbeing.

Focus on how it feels to live your best life.

You may not have achieved all of your goals or executed all of your dreams, but you do know what it would feel like to live your best life! When you focus on the feeling of living your best life, you don't have to have all of the answers or know the path to get there. Reassess personal values and aspirations to make sure your goals still align with your desires. Get rid of the distractions that displaced your focus to begin

90

with. Once you focus on achieving your goals and cut out the rest of the noise, you will be on a path of fulfillment.

Some situations that the *recognize, protect, and focus method* works great on: self-doubt, negative thinking, external situations out of your control, work or family stress, and burnout. Once you master the process, it may only take the *recognize* phase for you to realize that the discontent is here and gone in seconds because you know your boundaries and will remove yourself from situations that steal your peace. At that point, you've already refocused back on your happy, fulfilled, best life!

Living your best life is not a destination but a continuous process of self-discovery and growth. Embrace the fluidity of the journey and remember that it is okay to make adjustments and course corrections along the way using the recognize, protect, and focus methodology. Remember to celebrate your progress, no matter how small, and cultivate gratitude for the present moment which will only attract more joy into your life. Now that you've been armed with the tools for a passion-filled life, I know that you are on your way to living your best life!

Chapter Thirteen

Six Strategies for Living Your Best Life
By Karen McDonald

K aren McDonald, is CEO, Founder and Visionary of Wise Owl Legal Practice Management Software for Law Firms, has been involved in law firm accounting software support for over 25 years. This certainly has earned her the title of "The Wise Owl"!

Karen has an Accounting Degree and a passion for best use of technology. She is forever figuring how to use technology to improve efficiency and productivity and has many tales to tell. Like many of us, she has been through the pain of a divorce and survived, becoming stronger and wiser! She has worked in the world of accounting and accounting software including roles in accounting firms, government and industry.

Her all time favourite business book is 7 Habits of Highly Effective People.

Karen lives in Brisbane Queensland Australia with husband Bill. Away from the computer, she loves Smokey, her Maltese Shih Tzu, waterfalls and the outdoors!

www.linkedin.com/in/karen-mcdonald-697127

www.instagram.com/wiseowllegal

www.facebook.com/karen.mcdonald.313

www.wiseowllegal.com.au

www.karenmcdonald.online

Six Strategies for Living Your Best Life

By Karen McDonald

Life is a Celebration; Everyday is a Choice.

I am the driver. I am the end result of my many choices made day by day until today.

We all start with the same stuff. Yes, we have various "good" and "bad" things happen as children and then later...

How we choose how we respond and move on from such events is up to us. This is exactly how we see children of disadvantaged people rise to amazing success and children of the rich and famous die of drug overdoses.

Every day is a new day and I choose to celebrate each new day. Some days we can do special things like greet the sunrise. Many days that celebration is just "getting on with it." Whatever the day, a mindset of celebration of the day helps things appear anything but mundane.

Just this week I have been reminded about how precious and fragile life is. Two days ago, my 85 year old Mum had surgery for 3.5 hours to remove bowel cancer. We have now found out that without that surgery, she could have only lived another 6 months. Yes, life is precious. Value every day.

Workwise, I have only had one job I didn't enjoy. I wanted to leave in week 1, which was really odd for me. I stuck it out and left at the end of six very long months. After that, I promised myself that if I ever felt like that again about anything, I would not continue.

What is Your Best Life?

Our best life is uniquely different for each of us.

To understand what our best life is, we need to clearly understand our unique personal values. These values encompass all the dimensions of our lives. These values cover the emotional, spiritual, health, our physical well being, wealth, material things, and our legacy. Some of these things are dealt to us, others we have choices on how to craft ourselves.

Relationships with others are another paramount part of our best life. Having healthy relationships with others can be extremely rewarding. However, like everything there are healthy relationships and toxic ones and many others in between. I value my inner circle of relationships highly. It is great to have various people around us that all help us in different ways to be our best selves.

The late great Stephen Covey in his book, *The Seven Habits of Highly Effective People*, looks at what he calls our "centre." He supports living a "principal centred" life. Becoming aware of that philosophy in the early 1990's is something I have truly embraced and treasured. That philosophy has certainly stayed with me. Each of us needs to find our own core philosophy. The earlier in our lives we find this the better. I found the work I did around philosophies in the 1990's the most valuable of all the study I have done.

A thirst for knowledge is helpful to living your best life. An active mind keeps us focussed, an inquiring mind keeps us moving forward. Learning from the best and worst in life as we are meandering through this life enables us to move forward to bigger and better - in whatever bigger and better looks like to us. Over the years, many people have commented on my "inquiring mind". The main thing I know is that I am not capable of doing nothing!

Grateful

What are you grateful for today?

I am especially grateful for nature. As I write this I am reminded of how much more time I need to spend outdoors in nature. Nature really grounds me and brings me back to centre.

Over the years, especially as a single mother, I often gave thanks for my health.

As a single parent with 100% care responsibilities and little support in those child rearing years, I regularly expressed gratitude for my health, for being able to earn a living and to be able to provide for my children.

I have regularly given thanks for my ability to earn a living and support myself.

Strategies to Help Live My Best Life

Goals and Plans

I have always been a very goal-oriented person. I can recall patterns in the 1990's where I found myself sitting on my bed on a January Sunday morning, picking up a pad and writing furiously, without having planned to do so, and then realising I had just written out my goals for the year ahead. After this situation occurred spontaneously for about three years running, the lightbulb went off to realise my need for goals, especially for the new year, was part of my core being!

When something goes wrong, the first thing I do is make a plan on how to move forward. If I have a plan, I know what the next step is. A wise person, Benjamin Franklin, once said "If you fail to plan, you are planning to fail!"

There are lots of fun things we can do in our wonderful world and we should absolutely embrace them. Yes, when anyone asks me what I would tell my 20 or 30 year younger self, the answers are always the same: "Have more fun" and "Travel when you can, especially, when you are young." As much as I love my goals and plans, I have put "being responsible" before my dreams on way too many occasions.

Responses and Personal Boundaries

One of the things I have learned in the years is how the biggest choice we have each and every day is our response to every situation we are confronted with. Our sum choices of our responses shape our values which in turn shapes who we are. When confronted with a situation, we often don't realise in the moment but we have a myriad of choices.

Those choices have a massive impact on both ourselves and those around us. For example, it might seem foreign to some, but we truly do have a choice about whether we let a situation make us angry. This, I have learned first hand. Getting angry at a situation really does backfire and hurt ourselves more than anyone else. We do have a choice in our response. Always.

In more recent years, I have consciously worked on my emotional response to someone doing the wrong thing by me.

One example is people who "do me wrong". In the past I would sometimes become angry and or emotional and that anger would hurt me internally so much that my skin would break out in painful psoriasis. I was a slow learner (and am still learning) but have finally realised how I need to stand my ground, call the behaviour and then decide if there is appropriate action to address the situation and how to manage my own personal boundaries.

I have long heard about personal boundaries. Setting them effectively is sometimes a lot harder than the definition might imply. Walking the fine line of maintaining personal boundaries but not becoming an island is a complex balancing act.

Inner Circle

The inner circle of who we let into our world is very important. To work effectively, relationships must be two way. We contribute to those around us and those people contribute to us. Whilst our close relationships should not be a scorekeeping exercise, if the relationship is only one way of one person giving and the other person taking it, won't sustain. Having a trusted inner circle is a security blanket that I find essential.

Interestingly there are times and seasons for relationships. Some relationships simply peter out, others bring sadness as time moves on. Trusting the cycle of time and seasons helps us weather these changes in life.

Self Care

I grew up being taught that being selfish was evil. As I came into adulthood, especially in my mid 20's where others started depending on me, I realised that belief no longer served me. If others were depending on me for things essential to their lives, then my self care was crucial to being able to deliver what is needed. This is most emphasised when you are the carer for young children.

Self care matters. This is not to be confused with self indulgence and the crazy emotions when a person develops an "entitled" mind-set. Self care is taking time to recharge and keep our internal batteries charged. Yes, good sleep is fundamental for all of us. For me, self care includes the very important focus of being in nature regularly and recharging sitting in front of a flowing waterfall. What is self care for you?

Parent Yourself

The "parent yourself" concept from the 1990's is also a big support in getting on track / staying on track when it comes to mental health issues. So often our mind plays tricks on us and "remember-ing" to parent ourselves can certainly help us short circuit some of those rabbit holes. We also need to ensure that we have a great support network around us so that we can bounce ideas and strategies off each other. Whilst I am very self directed, I also find a lot of value in bouncing ideas off people I respect. Talking out our feelings and emotions with those in our inner circle can be very therapeutic.

Mistakes

Mistakes are an interesting part of your best life. Yes, we all make mistakes. The key is how we respond to them. We can choose to let them crush us or we can choose to learn from them. Finding the learning in a mistake is often a pivotal part of moving forward from a mistake.

Everyday Is a New Day

Yes, everyday is a new day! As an early riser, I have always been one to jump out of bed "bright-eyed and bushy-tailed" ready to embrace the new day.

We all get busy and can get overwhelmed by the busy-ness of life. However, each day is ours and how we choose to spend it is an opportunity we need to seize each day.

Each morning we have the opportunity to reset our world and start afresh! I encourage you, too, to celebrate each new day. Sunrise is my favourite time of day. What is your favourite time of day?

Chapter Fourteen

Building Your Positive People Network (PPN©)

By Dr. Kelly Ann Smith

D r. Kelly Ann Smith is a seasoned professional with three decades of experience in the Information Technology industry. Throughout her career, she has held both tactical and strategic roles, with the most recent emphasis on Project Management and Project Tooling.

Currently, Dr. Smith serves as a Senior IT Manager at a prominent bank in Tampa, Florida. Her expertise extends beyond her corporate role, as she is also an Adjunct Professor at a local community college, where she brings her real-world experience into the classroom to inspire and educate future professionals.

www.linkedin.com/in/drkellyannsmith

Building Your Positive People Network (PPN©)

By Dr. Kelly Ann Smith

Cultivating a "Positive People Network" (PPN©) has been a transformative journey in my pursuit of living my best life. My PPN is a close-knit group of personal, social, educational, religious, and professional connections who play a crucial role in supporting my mental well-being. This network has become an indispensable asset in my quest to achieve holistic wellness and personal growth.

While I've always prioritized my physical health through vitamins, proper nutrition, and exercise, I realized that my mental well-being required equal attention. Our emotional, psychological, and social health significantly impact how we think, feel and act, making it essential to nurture our mental well-being proactively.

Recognizing the profound effect of our connections on our lives, I made a conscious decision to surround myself with people who inspire personal growth and embody the character traits that contribute to making me a better person. I will share the steps I took to build my PPN, the core character traits I prioritized, and the continued efforts required to maintain and enrich this network. My hope is that others find inspiration to embark on their own path of personal growth and well-being.

The first step in my journey towards building a PPN was to document my aspirations and set clear goals. To achieve this, I outlined several key objectives:

1. Expand my interests and social circle to foster varied connections.
2. Remove toxic influences in my life, creating a positive environment.
3. Build supportive and trusting relationships that inspire personal growth.

4. Connect with individuals from diverse backgrounds and cultures to broaden my perspectives.

5. Expand my professional network to gain knowledge and expertise in a specific area.

Setting these personal goals provided clarity and purpose. I understood the direction I wanted to head and it increased my chances for success and growth.

Next, I identified my passions-the activities that brought me immense joy and fulfillment. Identifying and pursuing our passions are crucial components of building a PPN. Whether it was volunteering at a food bank, walking serene nature trails, reading my Bible, enjoying leisurely trips to the beach, embarking on a boat to cruise the Caribbean, spending cherished moments with my family and friends, or striving to improve corporate culture and employee trust in the workplace---each passion was categorized into Community Service, Spiritual, Travel, Professional, Physical, or Social interests. The passions I identified acted as guiding lights, leading me towards like-minded individuals who shared my principles and values. However, I realized that it was not just about connecting with just anyone.

To build a truly meaningful and impactful PPN, I established six core character traits that I prioritized in the individuals I sought to include in my network:

1. **Trustworthiness:** A person who is dependable, credible, and truthful; someone I can rely on completely.

2. **Authenticity:** One who is true to themselves and encourages others to do the same, creating a safe and judgment-free environment.

3. **Optimism:** A person who focuses on seeing the good in every situation, maintaining a positive attitude even in challenging times.

4. **Empathy:** Someone who understands and supports without judgment, offering genuine compassion and understanding.

5. **Collaborative:** A person who values teamwork and willingly shares knowledge, resources, and opportunities for the greater good.

6. **Growth Mindset:** One who believes in continuous learning, personal development, and self-improvement, embracing new ideas and unafraid of failure.

While all six traits are desirable, I recognized that trustworthiness and authenticity were non-negotiable for any individual to be part of my PPN. Trustworthiness embodies the essence of reliability, integrity, and honesty, which are the cornerstones of any meaningful relationship.

When trust is established, it lays a solid foundation for a supportive environment, fostering mutual growth and development among the network's members. As the trust deepens, so does the strength of the connections we share.

Authenticity, on the other hand, is a rare and precious trait that I hold in the highest regard. It requires individuals to be genuinely true to themselves, fearlessly embracing their core beliefs and values. In a world where societal pressures often coax people into conformity, authentic individuals stand out as beacons of truth and sincerity. They create an atmosphere of acceptance and understanding, where everyone feels free to express themselves without fear of judgment.

Writing down this criterion helped bring focus, accountability, and provided a base for measuring my accomplishments. It also served as a compass, guiding me through the process of building and expanding my PPN.

The next step involved determining how I would progress and ensure success in establishing my PPN. I began by evaluating my current network, comparing individuals against my desired character traits. While some individuals aligned well with these traits, others did not entirely fit the criteria. Instead of immediately severing ties, I created boundaries and distanced myself. Over time, these natural drifts led those who did not align with my desired characteristics to veer onto different paths.

To expand my PPN, I strategized each passion one by one. For instance, my passion for improving corporate culture and employee trust in the workplace stemmed from my Doctorate dissertation work. I have dedicated years to understanding how to build a more collaborative and less hierarchical workplace. To connect with like-minded individuals, I joined networking groups, enrolled in training classes, and attended local conferences.

For the remaining passions, I used the same approach, seeking outlets that led me to individuals with similar interests. Attending in-person and online networking events, joining various clubs and organizations, engaging in mentorships, and finding volunteer opportunities became avenues for finding compatible connections.

I also realized that the process of growing my PPN need not be overly formal. Simple acts of being open, friendly, and taking time to genuinely connect with others, even during everyday activities like trips to the grocery store, could lead to meaningful conversations and connections.

Throughout this journey, I learned that building a strong PPN goes well beyond collecting contacts; it is all about fostering sincere and meaningful connections that contribute to improving health and well-being.

The size of a PPN can differ for each person, yet the cognitive limit proposed by anthropologist Robin Dunbar of no more than 150 significant social relationships resonates with me. The concept reinforces the idea that emphasis should be placed on quality vs quantity.

Maintaining a strong PPN takes as much effort as building one. It is crucial not to assume that once a meaningful connection is established, it will remain meaningful forever. To preserve the value of a PPN connection requires continuously displaying the desired character traits and validating mutual worthiness.

Effective communication plays a vital role in maintaining a strong PPN and offering positive affirmations to PPN connections ensures they feel valued, capable, deserving, and uplifted. Hearing positivity triggers hormones like dopamine, endorphins, oxytocin, and serotonin, contributing to feelings of happiness, well-being, and inspiring emotions.

As life evolves, passions and priorities may shift. For instance, this year marked my transition to an "empty nester," and some of the passions I held when my kids were in school are no longer as relevant. Consistent reflection on goals and passions is essential, ensuring alignment with my desired path.

Assessment of my progress towards success involves a simple consistent review of the list of goals to ensure they align with my expectations. While we may always have control over external factors such as workplace dynamics, family situations, or broader societal issues, we have the power to control the company we keep. We can actively choose the people we surround ourselves with, nurturing relationships that profoundly influence our outlook on life, attitudes, and personal development. These connections with family, friends, and colleagues play a crucial role in shaping our mental well-being.

Building a Positive People Network is a lifelong journey—one that I cherish deeply. Each person in my PPN looks out for one another, offering support and encouragement in various aspects of life. Together, we strive to be the best versions of ourselves, motivating and uplifting each other to reach new heights.

I encourage each person to reflect on their own PPN journey. Through building a robust PPN, you'll not only enhance your well-being but also become part of a community that uplifts and empowers each other to embrace life's journey with greater joy and fulfillment. Seek out those who bring out the best in you, who believe in your potential, and who support your aspirations. Surround yourself with those that inspire you to "live your best life".

Chapter Fifteen

Maximizing Productivity
by Esther Maina

There is nothing more thrilling than being an integral part of someone else's success story. As a High-Ticket Coach and Closer, as well as an author, Esther Maina has been steering individuals to their next phase of life in both professional and personal aspects. While her extensive experience and knowledge are her biggest strengths, she believes success augments when you help others achieve their goals. Since then, she has never stopped working on building foundations for people to find a purpose-driven and successful life.

Growing up in Kenya, Esther was the middle child between two brothers. After holding a career in healthcare, she landed in a network company as a sales representative, trainer, and motivational speaker. Her journey in the USA started without any friends and family, and with a discovery about her pregnancy. While she has had her own fair share of challenges, she owes everything to her personal experience and certain career pivots. It was something that redefined her perspectives and made her way to Coach and Closer.

Driven by her keen insight into human behavior, she has been able to understand individuals from a unique vantage point and has steered others to reach their dreams with a clear vision and direction. While counselors and mentors assist clients to see what they are lacking in life, she believes in creating a roadmap to overcome her clients' obstacles in an effective way that provides real solutions with direct guidance.

Today, her mission is to provide each person with a one-of-a-kind strategy that is tailored for their dreams, so that they can carry out the plan with ease while they have her as the backbone of this journey. Throughout the process, she works to create a thought-provoking process that inspires one to reach higher and maximize their fullest potential personally and professionally.

While she believes that discovering a purpose and setting out to make it a reality is of paramount importance, she constantly works on achieving those for her clients, no matter what it takes. Whether it's closing a high-ticket deal as a business owner or influencer, or looking for a partner to work closely with you to facilitate your development, Esther is always here to help you get there.

www.linkedin.com/in/esthermainano1closercoach
www.instagram.com/esiimaina
www.facebook.com/profile.php?id=100082764521472
www.esthermaina.com

Maximizing Productivity

by Esther Maina

Environment Always Wins Over Will Power

In today's fast-paced world, where productivity is the holy grail of success, we all strive to accomplish more in less time. We set ambitious goals, make to-do lists, and try our best to stay focused and determined. But let's be honest, how many times have you found yourself struggling to meet those productivity targets? You're not alone!

Despite our best intentions and willpower, there's a hidden force at play that often tips the scales - our environment. The environment we find ourselves in has a profound impact on our productivity levels. It's like having a secret productivity ally or nemesis working silently behind the scenes. We can either let it destroy our ambitions or learn to harness it.

Boosting productivity is no easy feat, but it all starts with focusing on our environment. It's like a puzzle with multiple pieces that need to fit together perfectly. These are some of those key pieces: our physical space, the people we interact with, the technology we use, the information we absorb, and the habits we develop. Each of these elements plays a role in shaping our productivity landscape.

By paying attention to these elements, we can design an environment that empowers us to reach our productivity goals. It's all about creating a space that nurtures our growth and propels us towards success. The first step is recognizing what makes a strong environment, and how to avoid a weak one.

The Power of Environment

When it comes to productivity, the environment we operate in holds significant sway over our abilities. It subtly but powerfully influences our behaviors, habits, and ultimately, our levels of productivity. To grasp its impact, envision a spectrum stretching from the weakest environment on one end to the strongest on the other. At one extreme, the weakest environment comprises circumstances that hinder productivity, while at the opposite end, the strongest environment is purposefully crafted to foster and enhance productivity.

In the perpetual battle between personal willpower and environment, it is the environment that emerges victorious time and time again. This is not to diminish the importance of personal willpower, but rather to emphasize the profound influence that our surroundings have on it. No matter how resolute our willpower may be, if our environment fails to support productivity, we will find ourselves struggling to attain our full potential.

Consider a scenario where you are attempting to work in a cluttered and chaotic space, constantly bombarded by distractions. Your personal willpower may be robust, but the overwhelming environment constantly pulls your focus away from the task at hand. In such circumstances, maintaining high levels of productivity becomes a daunting challenge. On the other hand, if you operate within an environment thoughtfully designed to cultivate productivity, you will find it easier to maintain focus, sustain motivation, and accomplish your goals.

The power of the environment lies in its ability to shape our surroundings, optimize our workflow, and create the conditions necessary for productivity to thrive. It encompasses various aspects, including the physical space we occupy, the people we surround ourselves with, the technology we utilize, the information we consume, and the habits we develop. All of these elements come together to create an ecosystem that either nurtures or hinders our productivity.

By acknowledging the supremacy of the environment, we gain insight into the critical role it plays in our quest for productivity. It becomes evident that solely relying on personal willpower is not enough to overcome the obstacles posed by an unsupportive environment. Instead, we must consciously engineer our surroundings to align with our productivity goals. By doing so, we create an ecosystem that empowers us, enhances our capabilities, and sets the stage for success.

Designing a Productivity-Enhancing Environment

Creating a productivity-enhancing environment requires a deep understanding of its influence on us and a proactive approach to shaping it accordingly. By focusing on the following key areas, we can design an environment that optimally supports our productivity goals:

1. Physical Workspace: Our physical surroundings have a profound effect on our productivity. A cluttered and disorganized workspace can distract and impede our ability to concentrate. It creates mental and visual clutter that hinders our focus and efficiency. Conversely, a clean and well-organized environment can create a sense of calm and focus.

Ensure your workspace is free from distractions, well-lit, and tailored to your specific needs. Invest in ergonomic furniture that supports good posture and comfort. Organize your supplies efficiently, keeping frequently used items within reach. Personalize your space with motivational quotes, plants, or artwork that inspire and energize you. By optimizing your physical workspace, you create an environment that promotes productivity and enhances your overall well-being.

2. People: The company we keep plays a significant role in shaping our lives and well-being. Surrounding ourselves with supportive, encouraging, and like-minded individuals can have a profound impact on our productivity and overall happiness. Colleagues who offer support and motivation create a nurturing environment where creativity and collaboration can flourish. When ideas are met with encouragement and challenges are tackled collectively, it fosters a sense of empowerment and value within the group. This positive atmosphere leads to increased productivity and a more fulfilling work experience.

Conversely, spending time with people who engage in gossip and harbor negativity can be detrimental. Toxic environments drain energy and hinder progress, leading to reduced productivity and increased stress. Choosing to surround ourselves with positive and motivated individuals creates an uplifting atmosphere where everyone can thrive. Shared passions and ambitions lead to strong bonds, fostering camaraderie and mutual growth.

3. Technology: In today's digital age, technology plays a central role in our lives. It can be a powerful productivity tool, but it can also be a significant source of distraction. Take control of your technology use by minimizing non-essential notifications that interrupt your focus. Create designated work hours free from digital distractions, such as social media or personal emails. Use productivity-enhancing apps and tools to streamline your tasks and manage your time effectively.

Leverage technology to automate repetitive tasks, delegate responsibilities, and enhance collaboration with colleagues. However, be mindful of setting boundaries with technology. Establish clear guidelines for its usage, such as refraining from checking work emails outside of designated hours. By managing technology effectively, you create an environment where it serves as a tool to support your productivity rather than hinder it.

4. Information Consumption: The information we consume on a daily basis can shape our mindset and influence our productivity. Be intentional about the content you engage with. Seek out educational resources, inspiring literature, and podcasts that motivate and stimulate your productivity. Surround yourself with information that aligns with your goals and values.

Curate your social media feeds, following accounts and communities that offer valuable insights and inspiration. Unfollow or mute accounts that do not contribute positively to your growth. Subscribe to newsletters and blogs that provide valuable knowledge and industry updates. Allocate dedicated time for focused learning and personal development. By filtering out negative or irrelevant information and actively seeking out content that adds value, you create an environment that fosters knowledge, growth, and productivity.

5. Daily Habits: Our habits dictate our productivity on a subconscious level. By consciously designing and implementing productive habits, we can create an environment that supports our goals. Develop a routine that includes regular breaks, exercise, healthy eating, and sufficient sleep. Incorporate mindfulness or meditation practices to enhance focus and reduce stress. These habits will optimize your physical and mental well-being, leading to increased productivity.

Use time management techniques such as prioritizing tasks, using to-do lists, and setting realistic goals. Break large tasks into smaller, manageable steps to maintain momentum and motivation. Embrace the Pomodoro Technique, where you work in focused sprints followed by short breaks. By establishing positive habits and routines, you create an environment that encourages discipline, focus, and consistent productivity.

In the journey towards productivity, it is vital to acknowledge the significant influence of our environment. While personal willpower plays a crucial role, it is ultimately molded by the context in which we operate. By consciously designing our surroundings to support and enhance productivity, we establish a solid foundation for success. This involves carefully selecting the people we surround ourselves with, creating an organized and conducive workspace, effectively managing technology, curating the information we consume, and cultivating productive habits. By doing so, we construct an empowering environment that drives us towards our productivity goals.

It is essential to remember that the environment always emerges victorious, exerting a powerful influence on our actions and outcomes. By adopting a mindful approach to our surroundings, we unlock our full potential and flourish both personally and professionally. Our environment becomes the catalyst that propels us forward, fostering a harmonious alignment between our aspirations and the conditions that nurture our productivity.

With a conscious effort to shape our environment, we can harness its inherent power, amplify our abilities, and achieve heightened levels of productivity. By recognizing that the environment is a decisive factor in our success, we can take intentional steps to create an environment that inspires, supports, and motivates us. Let us embrace this understanding and actively create an environment that cultivates productivity, enabling us to thrive and reach our fullest potential in all areas of our lives.

Chapter Sixteen

Embracing Life After Loss
By Andrea Milner

Are you feeling lost and alone in the midst of heartbreak and loss? Andrea Evanson Milner knows exactly how you feel. She has experienced her own devastating losses, and now she's passionate about helping others navigate their own personal heartache.

As a grief transformation coach and certified grief educator, Andrea is here to support women like you. She'll guide you through the process of embracing your new identity and finding new meaning and purpose in life. With Andrea by your side, you'll gain clarity and confidence and learn how to take actionable steps without fear, overwhelm, or guilt.

Andrea offers a personalized coaching experience, where you'll have a safe space to explore your emotions and future goals. She also organizes transformative healing and discovery retreats. Imagine being surrounded by a nurturing environment filled with other women who understand your journey.

These retreats are designed to be powerful and enriching. You'll engage in therapeutic activities, have time for reflection and rejuvenation, and connect with like-minded individuals who are on a similar path to healing, growth, and discovery.

Andrea is committed to walking this healing journey with you. Her unwavering compassion and personal transformation make her the perfect guide to help you confidently and courageously live forward. Together, you'll embrace your new chapter with peace, hope, and renewed purpose. You don't have to go through this alone - Andrea is here for you.

www.linkedin.com/in/andrea-evanson-milner-604411157

www.instagram.com/iamandreaevansonmilner

www.facebook.com/andrea.evansonmilner

www.healgrowdiscover.com

Embracing Life After Loss

By Andrea Milner

Life is a journey filled with joy, love, excitement, wonder, and inevitably, loss. As everyday women, we navigate a myriad of experiences and emotions, and one of the most profound and challenging is grief. Unfortunately, we are bound to face heartbreaking losses that shatter our world and leave us feeling overwhelmed, lost, alone, and unsure of how to carry on. I understand the depths of this pain all too well, as I have walked the path of grief myself.

In this chapter, we will explore the path to healing after a significant loss — a journey that acknowledges our emotions and builds a strong support network, prioritizes self-care, and embraces courage and hope. Through these steps, we can find the clarity, strength, and confidence to move forward, while honoring the memory of our loved one and also honoring our emotions as we re-discover the beauty of life after loss.

Acknowledging Your Emotions

Grief is a natural and profound response to loss and no one can tell you how or when to grieve. Unfortunately, we live in a society that wants to avoid talking about grief and death while also trying to rush you through your grief by saying things like "get over it already," or "don't you think it's time to let go?" As a griever, these phrases are not comforting.

What we do need is to have our emotions and feelings witnessed and validated. Understanding grief is essential to our healing. It is not a linear process with a definitive end point. Instead, it unfolds uniquely for each individual. With grief, there is never a timeline, so you need to be patient with yourself and give yourself the space to grieve in your own way and at your own pace. Only you know what is best for you. Some days will feel overwhelming, while others may offer a glimmer of hope.

When we acknowledge our emotions and allow ourselves to experience and process the stages of grief, we begin to heal. Understand that it is okay to feel anger, sadness, guilt, denial, and even shame. One minute, you might be crying and saying, "I can't believe this is happening to me," and the next minute you might be angry at your loved one and shouting "why did you have to go so soon?"! Each emotion is valid and a necessary part of the healing process. We need to embrace these feelings as a testament to the love shared. Grief will never fully go away but there will come a day when you will be able to move forward with more love than pain.

 What we have once enjoyed deeply we can never lose. All that we love deeply becomes a part of us.

— Helen Keller

Creating a Support Network

Healing from grief is not a solo journey. Even if you want to stay in bed all day and shut out the world, you still need to be able to express all your feelings and emotions. Creating a support network of understanding and compassionate individuals can make all the difference.

Surround yourself with family members and friends who are willing to listen without judgment. It can even be extremely helpful connecting with a total stranger that has experienced a similar situation. There are many support groups out there also, whether it's in person or an online community.

It is crucial to set healthy boundaries during your healing process. Recognize when you do need some time alone to process your emotions and communicate these needs to your support network. A healthy support system will respect your boundaries and offer support when you are ready to open up. There will be people that want to be there for you but just don't know what to say or what to do so you have to be willing to ask for help if you need it. Just having someone pick up your mail, take out your garbage, pick up a few groceries, or drop off some food can make a huge difference. In grief, asking for help is not a sign of weakness, it's a necessity. And remember: you are not broken, you don't need fixing, what you do need is knowing there is someone you can call on at any time to listen and provide comfort during your darkest days.

 The internal work of grief is a process, a journey. It does not have prescribed dimensions and it does not end on a certain date.

— David Kessler

Prioritize Self Care

In the midst of grief, especially in the early stages, self-care may feel like an afterthought, but it is a vital aspect of the healing process. I know it's difficult to get motivated at times, but you have to make a conscious decision to eat, stay hydrated, and get some fresh air. Nurturing your body, mind, and soul is essential for your overall well-being. Now is the time to take care of yourself more than ever.

Here Are a Few of My Self-Care Favorites

- **Mindful breathing** — practicing deep breathing exercises can help to reduce stress and promote relaxation.
- **Guided Meditation** — grief is so emotionally draining so you need to get quality sleep to recharge. However when you can't sleep, guided meditation can be a game changer.

- **Read an Uplifting Book or Watch a Funny Movie** — books and movies can inspire, lift you up, and make you laugh.
- **Journaling** — is such a great way to reflect on what you are grateful for even in the midst of grief. Cultivating gratitude can provide some perspective and peace.
- **Physical Activity** — a walk around the block, simple stretching, or some gentle yoga helps to release tension and anxiety and releases those feel good endorphins. Oh and 1 more, turn up the music and dance like nobody's watching!

Show yourself love and compassion during this journey. You need to treat yourself with care and understanding. I invite you to find a photograph of yourself as a young child, preferably under 5 years old. How do you see this child? How would you talk to this child? It's a powerful exercise when you are being too hard on yourself. Please be kind to yourself as you navigate the complexities of grief.

 We tend to judge ourselves harshly. In grief, we would never talk to others in the same harsh tones and with the same words we talk to ourselves.

— Louise Hay

Moving Forward With Courage and Hope

There will come a time when you cry a little bit less, and feel a little more hopeful. While grief never fully dissipates, we eventually learn to carry it alongside the beautiful memories of our loved one. Embrace gratitude for the time you shared and the memories that will forever be treasured in your heart. Accept the healing journey as a transformative process. Ask yourself what do I want to be, do, or have? Moving forward after loss does not mean forgetting or leaving the past behind but incorporating it into your life in a way that honors the memory of your loved one.

Here are a few signs and indicators that can help you determine if you are moving towards readiness to embrace life's new chapter:

- **Emotional Awareness** — while you may still experience moments of sadness and grief, you notice you are also experiencing moments of comfort and peace.
- **Acceptance of Reality** — you have started to accept the reality of the loss and understand that your loved one is physically no longer with you.
- **Shift in Perspective** — you may notice a shift in how you view the world and your place in it. While the loss remains a part of your life, you are open to exploring new possibilities and finding meaning in your experiences.
- **Engagement of Activities** — you find yourself engaging in activities and hobbies that you used to enjoy before the loss. You may also discover new interests and passions that bring a sense of fulfillment.
- **Increased Energy and Motivation** — you feel more energized and motivated to take steps towards your future. This could include setting goals, making plans, or pursuing personal growth opportunities.

There will still be waves of grief even when you feel you are moving forward. Give yourself permission to feel whatever emotions come up and take the time you need to heal. Trust in yourself, and in your strength as you navigate your journey of healing and growth.

As everyday women, we are strong, resilient, and capable of healing from the deepest wounds. The path to healing after significant loss requires acknowledging our pain, building a strong support network, prioritizing self-care, and moving forward with courage and hope. Remember, it's okay to grieve and to take all the time you need. Your journey is unique, and healing will unfold in its own time.

By acknowledging your emotions, reaching out for support, and nurturing yourself with love and compassion, you will discover that you can move forward gently while cherishing the memories of your loved one. Honor the past while growing and embracing the future with courage and hope. You are a beautiful, extraordinary woman with so much to give in this world, and I believe in you.

 Pay attention to the things you are naturally drawn to. They are often connected to your path, passion, and purpose in life. Have the courage to follow them.

— Ruben Chavez

Chapter Seventeen

Love Saves

By Jacqueline Colon

J acqueline Colon is a Behavioral Health Therapist with a Bachelor's Degree in Behavioral Science. She was born and raised in the Bronx, NY., now resides in Connecticut with her two youngest of four amazing children. She is working on building her business JC Blessings 4 U LLC. She is passionately committed to supporting women to live their lives to their fullest potential and embrace their power and purpose. By doing that, they create vision boards — a collage of images, pictures, and affirmations of one's dreams and desires. Each design is to serve as a source of inspiration and motivation to attain one's goal. She leads, inspires, and mentors women through her motto: *TEAM- Together Everyone Achieves More.*

She's partnered up with Modern Nature and created her second online business, earning an income from her phone. She is a hair/skin & wellness consultant helping women feel and look great. They are the only anti-aging hair care line in the world, and the #1 fastest growing luxury hair care company in North America. The products they offer are 100% vegan, gluten-free, and Leaping Bunny Certified! Natural based products that are clinically backed & proven to grow the hair & reverse damage to its healthiest state with no chemicals, sulfates, parabens, or harmful fragrances.

www.linkedin.com/in/sheisblessed

www.instagram.com/transform_manifest_execute

www.facebook.com/jacqueline.colon904

www.linktr.ee/blessings_4u

Love Saves

By Jacqueline Colon

BEAUTIFUL WOMEN
LISTEN!

" Any transition serious enough to alter your definition of self will require not just small adjustments in your way of living and thinking but a full-on metamorphosis.

— Martha N. Beck

They ask me: *"Why are you always there for others, even though you are not feeling well yourself?"*
My answer is: *"Because I know how it feels when everybody looks the other way."*

I am a single mother born and raised in the Boogie Down, Bronx. I have four amazing children whom I love with all my heart. I lost my dad, the pillar that held the family together, in 1996, at the age of 39, when I was only 17 years old. In January 2023, I lost my most precious jewel, my mom. Being an adult orphan has been challenging and the most difficult defeat I have faced. I am the oldest of three siblings. I am now left to care for my siblings and my children.

I have fought many battles which have led to low self-esteem, depression, and anxiety. I have kept all to myself. I was in a dark time in my life. I felt so alone, so empty, and hurt. I had no support, guidance, or anyone to converse with. I didn't know who to turn to or where to turn for support to get the LOVE that I yearned for.

Dysfunction becomes normal in your mind and it contaminates your character. It causes you to be misunderstood by others. It becomes a hidden character in your identity. Forgiving yourself and those who have caused your heart to be hardened will prevent you from remaining stagnant. There is strength in forgiveness. Allow my story to help you.

Let's start by falling in LOVE with yourself and taking care of you. Life is a voyage of self-discovery. To me, to be enlightened is to go within and learn who and what we really are, to know that we have the ability to change for the better by loving and taking care of ourselves.

Love is having a deep appreciation for who you are. I have found that the most simple things are the most profound. We are the power we have been seeking. The power that has created this universe has often been referred to as love. God is love. We have often heard the statement, "Love makes the world go 'round." It's all true. LOVE is the key that holds the universe together.

I found myself running to God, the only person I know that can deliver me from the fractures and instability that were taking over my mind. As a child who grew up going to service on Sundays as a family, and seeing my parents so highly involved with the community and their spirituality, I knew through God I would find what I longed for. I knew through God I wasn't going to be judged and would receive the LOVE I needed. I found deliverance in God and allowed him to reconstruct my mind, body, & soul. Now, I'm free from bondage! My wings were spread wide open and that's how I became a beautiful butterfly embracing a life of transformation. I was released from my limitations and negative beliefs.

I Have an Exercise for You

Stand in front of a mirror and recite the following at least six times:

"[Your name], I love you."
Gaze into your eyes as you say it, being meaningful while you deliver the words.
Avoid looking away or staring at what is behind you

126

through the mirror. Don't use the camera on your smartphone to do this exercise, let it be raw and simple.

Ok, try the exercise now.

What did you notice?
What feelings arose?
Could you hold your gaze and feel the words I love you?
Some people are in tears when doing this simple yet powerful exercise.
Let's be honest, if you cannot love yourself, how can you embrace the love of another person?
You are likely to feel unworthy while longing for the love and intimacy of another person.
That's where conflict arises.
When you love yourself, life takes care of the details. Everything else is minor compared to the acceptance of one's self.

Self-love and practicing self-care saved my life. We aren't taught this in school and I didn't come from a family that practiced nor educated me with these valuable tools, but I wanted more. There was always a burning humbleness and desire inside me to find a greater purpose to succeed, thrive and be my authentic self. This is when I started to put my visions, dreams and goals into manifestation through vision boarding. I used this process in 2018 and I accomplished my health and fitness goals. I was able to run a few half marathons and receive medals. I became an Insanity fitness instructor for the YMCA. I was a health and fitness assistant coach with a well-known personal trainer from Yonkers, New York, where we held bootcamp sessions for women and ran a ninja warriors afterschool program for kids. Through these events, I met amazing people along the way. I was so much happier, healthier, and full of energy. I gained back my self-esteem. All of this came from the power of loving myself.

I now do vision boards yearly and help women create their own vision boards where they achieve and accomplish their goals, such as paying off a car, running in the Boston Marathon, or making reading a part of their routine.

When Covid-19 hit, I found myself moving towards bigger goals like moving away, buying a new car, and continuing my education. Those voices that once told me, "you are the devil's child," you're evil, you're just going to live off the system, everybody hates you," What was meant to scar me helped to build my metamorphosis. I used this time where the world was facing uncertainty to reconstruct myself because I loved myself enough to no longer allow harm in my life.

Sure enough, what I manifested on my vision board came into existence. I moved out of New York. I earned my Bachelor's degree in Behavioral Science. I work as a Behavioral Interventionist and am currently working on building my own business. The lockdown and the uncertainty of COVID-19 didn't stop me from achieving the goals I set for myself. Every time I passed my vision board, I heard a voice in my head say, "yes you can" and that voice pushed me even harder towards manifesting and meeting my goals. In March 2023, I did my first sip and zoom vision board event and hope to continue holding these events.

In order to live your best life, you must LOVE yourself, know your self-worth, know your value, and your strength. You are as strong as your mind. Your value is what you create. Your strength is dependent on God. I challenge you today to go over the exercise I provided you with a few times and dig deep into your inner soul and get to love who you really are and go conquer your dreams! I pray that my words will encourage you to walk by faith, and not by sight (2 Corinthians 5:7).

Chapter Eighteen

The Power of Intention and Surrender
By Jennifer Williams

M eet Jennifer Williams, a certified life and health coach who specializes in Attachment Theory and Dialectical Behavior Therapy. Jennifer is passionate about helping people make meaningful connections with themselves and others and empowering them to lead the lives they deserve.

With her unique blend of compassion and expertise, Jennifer provides a supportive space for her clients to discover their purpose and navigate personal growth. As an introverted individual, Jennifer has honed her intuitive listening skills and has a knack for recognizing her clients' true selves.

Jennifer's enthusiasm for life is contagious and evident in all that she does. She is a talented writer and enjoys channeling her creative energy into works of art. In her free time, she also likes to repurpose furniture as a fun hobby.

www.instagram.com/jens.life.coaching
www.facebook.com/jensLifeCoaching
www.Jenslifecoaching.com

The Power of Intention and Surrender

By Jennifer Williams

Get ready to have your mind blown in this epic chapter as I reveal the life-changing skills and wisdom that have completely transformed my own story.

If you're ready to take control of your life and start living your best life, then keep on reading.

As women, we constantly find ourselves facing various challenges in our daily lives. From balancing careers with family life to navigating so many relationships and dealing with self-doubt, the obstacles can sometimes seem never-ending.

What sets apart those who thrive from those who merely survive? It all boils down to a crucial set of life skills tailored to our individual journeys.

As I approach the halfway mark of my existence, I am struck by how the little girl in me still perceives 30 as old. Despite gaining wisdom over the years, I can't help but feel like a perpetual student of life. Like all of us, I am constantly navigating the ups and downs. And through this remarkable adventure called life, I've embraced certain skills and values that have paved my path to inner peace and genuine happiness.

I have narrowed it down to five core values everyone can benefit from and bonus skills that we all should know plenty about by now.

Live With Intention

Living with intention means having a clear and purposeful direction in your life. It's about being mindful of your actions, thoughts, and decisions, and aligning them with your values and beliefs. Intentional living helps you live in the present moment and make the most of every opportunity. It requires introspection, self-awareness, and courage to make intentional choices that may not always be easy or popular but are aligned with your goals and aspirations.

It's easy to get caught up in the hustle and bustle of daily life and lose sight of what truly matters. Intentional living forces us to slow down and reflect on what's important.

To live with intention, start by setting clear goals, identifying your values, and prioritizing your time and energy accordingly.

Establishing meaningful routines and prioritizing self-care have been the ultimate game changers in my life. Building better habits and living with intention can be achieved through the use of routines. This can start with a simple bedtime routine that sets us up for the next day or taking morning vitamins with our morning coffee.

Learn to say no to things that don't serve your highest good and focus on cultivating habits and relationships that do. Prioritizing our time and energy is essential for healthy living. One of the best ways of self-care is sometimes saying no.

It's also important to acknowledge that living with intention is not a one-time decision, but an ongoing process of self-discovery and growth.

Surrender to Control

By understanding your locus of control, you can unlock the key to living your best life. Locus of control refers to the extent to which you believe you have control over the events and outcomes in your life. It's a concept that plays a significant role in empowering yourself and seizing opportunities for change.

At its core, locus of control is divided into two categories: internal and external. Those with an internal locus of control believe that they have the power to shape their own destiny. They take responsibility for their actions and decisions, understanding that they hold the key to their own success.

On the other hand, individuals with an external locus of control tend to believe that outside forces, other people, their parents or luck determine their fate. They may feel powerless and attribute their failures or lack of progress to external factors.

Embracing an internal locus of control doesn't mean dismissing external factors entirely. It's important to recognize that not everything is within our control. However, by focusing on what we can influence and making the most of the opportunities that come our way, we can navigate change with confidence and purpose.

So, take a moment to reflect on your own locus of control. Do you tend to blame external factors for your successes and failures, or do you believe in your own ability to shape your destiny? Do you spend a lot of time worrying about the choices and behaviors of others? Do you become irritable sitting in traffic or dealing with stupid people? The answers may transform your life in ways you never thought possible.

Not Everyone is Our "Friend"

We often use the word "friend" so loosely that it loses its meaning. We refer to the people we work with, our classmates or even our neighbors as our friends. But the reality is that not everyone is our "friend". True friendship requires trust, shared values, and mutual support. It takes time and effort to cultivate. It's not a numbers game. Sure, there may be a bunch of people at your birthday bash, weekend BBQ or even your funeral, and they STILL are not all your friends. And that is okay.

As humans, we tend to place significant importance on the relationships we form. We all strive to be liked and valued by those around us. However, what happens when we try to force relationships that just don't quite fit? Or when we confide in someone who hasn't yet earned that privilege because we call them a "friend". Or when someone doesn't show up for us the way we expected? We can end up feeling hurt and disappointed by the other person's lack of interest or investment in us.

It's important to recognize that people may simply be acquaintances or colleagues or a friend of a friend or family member (family does not equal friends). Assigning others to the appropriate lane and not expecting more than they're capable of can help us avoid hurt and disappointment. We may not always be able to choose who comes into our lives, but we do have control over where we place them. By rethinking our approach to relationships and navigating the labyrinth with purpose, we can find ourselves surrounded by the people who genuinely support and uplift us.

By utilizing the relationship labyrinth (or the idea of compartmentalizing people in our lives), we can identify who belongs in what space and stop wasting time and energy trying to make connections that just aren't meant to be. It isn't a matter of good or bad people, but rather acknowledging where someone fits in our lives and respecting that space.

So when we use the label "friend," we need to think carefully about what it means. It's better to have a few genuine friends who have our backs when we need them than a large circle of acquaintances who are only there for the good times. So let's reserve the word "friend" for those who truly deserve it and appreciate their value in our lives. Let's not take the people who are always there for us for granted and treasure their friendship for the precious gift that it is.

Bonus. Master These Skills:

Ditch the Toxic Trio: gossiping, complaining, and a negative mindset - they're all energy vampires. These skills not only harm relationships, including the one we have with ourselves, but also reveal a lack of emotional intelligence.

Gossiping breeds negativity, destroying trust and nurturing shallow connections fueling drama and ruins self-esteem. It's just fancy chatter that lacks depth and empathy. Remember this: if they are gossiping with you, they are gossiping about you.

Constant **complaining** fixates our minds on the negative, achieving nothing and adding more fuel to the fire.

A **negative mindset** attracts more negativity.

Adopt the Magic Three: Positivity, forgiveness and gratitude. They are the antidotes for the toxic trio.

When we embrace **positivity,** we become magnets for more positivity. No matter how tough the day may be, we can face it with grace and acceptance, unburdened by the need to control everything. Embrace the magic of positivity and watch your world transform.

Forgiveness isn't just a nice gesture; it's essential for our personal growth and happiness. By choosing to forgive, we liberate ourselves from the heavy weight of grudges and bitterness. It allows us to heal, move forward, and create a brighter future.

Gratitude is the key to happiness. It's not the happy people who are grateful, but the grateful people who are happy. No matter how tough things get, there is always something to be grateful for.

To conclude, living our best life is a journey that we must continue to pursue. We must become mindful of our thoughts and feelings, embrace intention in how we choose to live, understand the power of control and accept that not everyone is meant to be in our lives.

It's crucial to create healthy boundaries with friends, family and colleagues because they each have their individual purposes in our lives. We should seek out people who will challenge us for growth, empower us when we feel down and also provide support when it's needed.

By understanding all these key takeaways, it can help create more abundant peace within ourselves and with those that are around us. Furthermore, it's important to remember that setting the right intentions for ourselves will allow us to achieve extraordinary success in anything we pursue as women.

Chapter Nineteen

How Elder Women Can Live Their Best Life
By Faten Shelbayeh

Faten Shelbayeh is a Palestinian-Jordanian-American writer. She began writing in 2017, her first book is *You Care ..We Care: Stop Elder Abuse.* She lives in Massachusetts, USA. Faten is a proud mother of two girls and a boy.

She has earned many high levels of education from well-known colleges and universities in the U.S. in multiple fields such as: financial management, healthcare administration, Autism Applied behaviours, education, and public policy. She speaks two Languages (Arabic and English).

Faten is passionate about helping elderly people within her community in Massachusetts and would love to expand all over the United States and the world.

Faten has been serving at Malden Human Rights Commission and managing an elderly home care agency since 2019 and providing training to caregivers to help them provide better services to people who need help in the comfort of their homes.

Faten is passionate about making a change within the community and helping others, especially those in need. She is a dedicated volunteer and fundraiser for many charitable organizations, such as Foodbank, and she is a member of many organizations, such as National Association of Social Workers for Economy, Peace, and Justice, International Society of Female Professionals, and National Writers Union.

She enjoys reading, writing, cooking, and sports in her spare time.
www.facebook.com/fshelbayeh?mibextid=LQQJ4d
www.faten78us-28098.gr8.com

How Elder Women Can Live Their Best Life

By Faten Shelbayeh

Women experience particular difficulties as they get older, which can make it hard for them to live their best lives. The state of one's mental and emotional health can be negatively impacted by physical changes, the death of loved ones, and societal expectations. However, older women can survive and relish their golden years with the appropriate mindset and techniques. In this chapter, we will look at strategies for older women to live their best lives and find happiness and fulfillment at every stage of their lives.

Ways Elder Women Can Live Their Best Live

Prioritizing Self-Care

Everyone needs to take care of themselves, but older women, who may have spent the majority of their lives taking care of others, especially so. In this chapter, we'll look at ways that older women can put their own needs first and look after their physical, mental, and emotional well-being. This includes advice on how to handle stress, eat a nutritious diet, get enough sleep, and keep active. They should also keep up with their routine medical exams and screenings, such as colonoscopies, mammograms, and testing for bone density.

Keeping Your Mind Sharp

Physical health maintenance and mental stimulation go hand in hand. To keep their minds active, older women might take part in reading, learning new skills, and puzzle solving. Additionally, avoiding cognitive decline can be aided by being social and upholding healthy relationships.

Staying Connected with Family and Friends

It's common to feel alone and distant from the people we care about as we get older. However, it is essential for our well-being to continue to have close ties to our family and friends.

Pursuing Your Passions and Hobbies

We don't have to stop following our interests and hobbies just because we get older. In actuality, engaging in hobbies and interests is a great way to stay active and involved in life. Senior women should discover new interests and hobbies to keep themselves motivated and interested. They can experiment with hobbies like gardening, painting, or volunteering, which can give them a sense of fulfillment and purpose.

Navigating Changes in Relationships

Relationships between older women and their family and friends may alter as they get older. While some people could lose something, others might make new connections. It's crucial to approach these changes with positivity and openness and to ask for help when you need it.

Embracing Self-Care

Self-care is an essential part of living one's best life. Elder women should prioritize activities that make them feel good, such as getting a massage, taking a relaxing bath, or practicing meditation. Additionally, they should practice self-compassion and avoid negative self-talk.

Staying Engaged with the World

Older women might feel connected and fulfilled by continuing to participate in the world around them. They can take part in neighborhood activities, join an organization or group, or volunteer for a cause they support.

Cultivating Strong Relationships

Strong relationships are essential for the social and emotional wellbeing of older women. By keeping in touch with loved ones, participating in social activities, and volunteering, they can maintain current relationships. By participating in novel activities and meeting like-minded individuals, they can also create new relationships.

Managing Finances and Retirement

In order to ensure that older women may live comfortably and safely as they approach retirement, it is crucial that they handle their funds carefully. They should establish a budget that enables them to live within their means and periodically examine their retirement funds. In order to develop a strategy for long-term financial stability, people should also think about consulting a financial counselor.

Maintaining Independence and Mobility

Maintaining independence and mobility is crucial for elderly women's quality of life. They can take steps to prevent falls, such as installing handrails and removing trip hazards from their homes. They can also explore mobility aids, such as canes or walkers, if necessary. Finally, they should consider transportation options that allow them to stay active and engaged with the world around them.

Cultivating a Positive Mindset

A positive mindset can greatly impact elderly women's well-being. They can practice gratitude by reflecting on the things they are thankful for each day. They can also challenge negative thought patterns by reframing them in a positive light. Additionally, they should surround themselves with positive people and avoid toxic relationships.

Exploring New Technologies

With the aid of new technologies, elderly women can stay engaged, informed, and connected. To stay in touch with family and friends, they can use social media. They can also experiment with new gadgets and apps that can make their lives more convenient. They can also obtain information and resources on vital subjects like finances and health via technology.

Common Challenges that Elderly Women Face

Women experience a range of obstacles specific to their gender as they get older. Senior women frequently struggle to preserve their independence and sense of identity due to a variety of factors, including changes in their physical and mental health and societal attitudes toward aging. In this booklet, we will examine some of the most prevalent problems that older women encounter and offer solutions.

Health Issues

Health problems are one of the biggest obstacles that elderly women must overcome. Women are more susceptible to health issues including osteoporosis, heart disease, and dementia as they get older. These ailments may have an impact on their day-to-day activities and make it challenging for them to complete tasks that they once found simple. Elderly women must take care of their physical health by getting regular exercise, eating a balanced diet, and keeping up with doctor visits.

Social Isolation

Another problem that elderly women frequently experience is social isolation. They might lose friends and loved ones as they get older, and their social circle might get smaller. This may result in depression and feelings of isolation. By engaging in social events, joining organizations, and keeping connections with friends and family, older women can stay socially active and engaged.

Financial Insecurity

An additional issue that a lot of elderly women deal with is financial uncertainty. They could not have a sizable retirement fund, which would make it challenging for them to pay for needs like housing, health care, and food. To make sure they have adequate means to support themselves in their later years, elderly women must make retirement plans and seek financial counseling.

Ageism

Ageism is a type of discrimination that affects elderly women a lot. They might not receive job offers, be patronized or disregarded in social settings, or be the target of unfavorable stereotypes. The significance that senior women contribute to society must be acknowledged, and ageist attitudes and actions must be challenged.

Caregiving

Many elderly women also have caring responsibilities, whether it is for their partners, kids, or other family members. Their personal health and wellbeing may suffer as a result of having such a demanding job, both physically and mentally. Elderly women must prioritize their own needs and enlist help from others when necessary.

In this chapter, we've looked at ways for elderly women to live their best lives and get past common obstacles that come with getting older. Elder women can thrive and enjoy their golden years by prioritizing self-care, maintaining mental acuity, maintaining relationships with loved ones, pursuing passions and hobbies, and making wise financial and retirement decisions. Additionally, people can maintain a sense of purpose and fulfillment by developing a positive outlook, utilizing new technologies, and keeping active in their surroundings.

It is crucial to recognize that when women age, they may have particular difficulties like health problems, social isolation, and financial uncertainty. However, these difficulties can be solved with the appropriate approaches and assistance. Elder women should put their physical, mental, and emotional health first in order to preserve healthy relationships and a sense of direction in their lives.

As a society, we must also acknowledge and solve the structural problems, such as ageism, sexism, and inadequate healthcare systems that contribute to the difficulties experienced by elderly women. We can build a world where elderly women may live their best lives and continue to contribute to their communities and society at large by adopting policies and attitudes that value and support them.

In conclusion, this chapter provides senior women with a roadmap for overcoming the particular difficulties they face and leading the greatest lives possible. Elder women can have fulfilling lives in their golden years by prioritizing self-care, staying in touch with loved ones, following passions and hobbies, and maintaining a positive outlook.

Chapter Twenty

5 Easy Questions For Living Your Best Life!
By Dr. Vicki Coleman

D r. Vicki D. Coleman is an internationally recognized Behavioral Health Specialist, Psychologist, Best Selling Author, Professor, Researcher, and Talk Show Host. A former Tenured Professor at Purdue University in West Lafayette, IN, she has also held positions at the State University of New York and American Airlines. As a researcher, she has refereed publications on counseling strategies, sports psychology, career development, addictions, and multicultural/diverse populations.

As President/CEO of The Coleman Group, she globally consults for education, business, industry, government, and professional associations. A native of Detroit, Michigan, Dr. Coleman earned Bachelor's and Master's degrees from The University of Iowa; a Master's from Northern Illinois University; and a Doctorate in Counseling Psychology from Rutgers University. As a Sports Psychologist working with student, professional, and retired athletes, she is also completing her sports certification in peak performance.

Dr. Vicki D. Coleman is Represented by Bruce Merrin, of the Bruce Merrin Celebrity Speakers & Entertainment Bureau.

www.linkedin.com/in/doccole

www.instagram.com/AngerDoctor

www.facebook.com/DrVickiDColeman

www.angerdr.com

5 Easy Questions For Living Your Best Life!

By Dr. Vicki Coleman

So, you want to "Live Your Best Life"?

And you can, by considering a response to the "5 Easy Questions" that will facilitate a better understanding of who you are, and what you want your life to be!

However, prior to answering the "5 Easy Questions", it is important to critically examine, analyze, and discuss your Self-Concept and Self-Esteem, as these two constructs are the foundational pillars of personal, family, professional, and financial success, among others.

SELF-CONCEPT AND SELF-ESTEEM

To begin living your best life, I believe, we should initially focus on Self-Concept and Self-Esteem.

Self-Concept is the perception that we have of ourselves; and Self-Esteem is how we "feel" about ourselves.

As Self-Concept and Self-Esteem are not one construct, based on my theoretical framework and orientation, I subscribe to and modified the 6 Areas of Self-Concept developed by Fitts & Warren (1964, 1996), and illustrated in their classic, global inventory, the Tennessee Self-Concept Scale (TSCS).

My Model of Self-Concept and Self-Esteem is listed below:

- Personal Self-Concept and Self-Esteem
- Physical Self-Concept and Self-Esteem
- Family Self-Concept and Self-Esteem
- Social/Community Self-Concept and Self-Esteem

- Academic/Work/Professional/Financial Self-Concept and Self-Esteem
- Moral/Ethical/Spiritual Self-Concept and Self-Esteem

Understanding my Model of the self in each of the above 6 Areas is the initial step in living your best life. One *must* identify the issues, concerns, and challenges related to *each* of the 6 Areas of Self-Concept and Self-Esteem; and ask yourself,

"Who am I?"

"What are the challenges that I have encountered throughout my life, including obstacles and barriers?"

"What are my short and long-term goals?; and more importantly,

"How do I want to live my best life?"

DEVELOPMENT OF THE 5 EASY QUESTIONS

Over the years, personally and professionally, I have observed a myriad of experiences concerning the "development" and cycle of relationships. And I have discerned that it is all in the "Admission Process", when we Allow individuals to enter our lives for consideration as a Boyfriend/Girlfriend/Partner/Spouse/Boo/Bae/Colleague, or whatever label we choose to call or identify the relationship.

While working as a contractor for the City of Las Vegas Municipal Court in its Alternative Sentencing and Education (ASED) Department, I facilitated several courses. ASED is an opportunity for individuals to participate in psychoeducational programs, rather than face jail or incarceration.

The courses that I facilitated for ASED included Domestic Violence for male and female perpetrators; Impulse Control; Anger Management; Substance Abuse; and the Driving Under the Influence (DUI) School. During this dynamic and engaging experience, I wanted to recommend an intervention that might build and enhance the communication skills of the participants.

Therefore, I developed the "5 Easy Questions", and later incorporated them into my private practice and educational endeavors, recommending them to clients, patients, family, friends, and colleagues, to name a few.

I strongly recommend that these questions be asked during the early encounters, not necessarily the First Engagement; however, early in the "Relationship!"

The "5 Easy Questions" can serve as the foundation for understanding ourselves as they pertain to the development of relationships, ultimately, facilitating living your best life. Also, the "5 Easy Questions" can be asked no matter the type of engagement or relationship, i.e., personal, family, professional, financial, collegial, or community, among others.

The "5 Easy Questions"

1. What Are Your Values? (Anything that is important to the individual, for example, family, education, financial security...)
2. What Are Your Core Beliefs? (Some believe that women should stay home with the children, if any, and that the men should provide all of the financial resources and security...)
3. How Do You Handle Anger and Conflict? (Anger is a valid emotion, and there will always be some level of conflict in relationships. However, what are the defense and coping mechanisms utilized to understand and regulate anger. There will always be conflict in our lives; and what strategies and techniques are considered for resolving conflict?)
4. What Are Your Short-Term Goals? (1-2 years)

5. What Are Your Long-Term Goals? (2+ years)

It is amazing the type of information that is revealed when one asks these "5 Easy Questions"!

Individuals have told me, personally and professionally, that it was these "5 Easy Questions" that helped them determine IF the "Encounter" should move to the next level, including assisting in identifying the criteria for living your best life.

The goal is that there should be congruence with self, and others; and also between the two, or more, individuals for a successful, caring, honest, loving, and healthy relationship.

LIVING YOUR BEST LIFE

Most would agree that relationships are important for living your best life.

Knowing who we are, with respect to Self-Concept and Self-Esteem, is a necessary foundation for living your best life.

And asking the "5 Easy Questions" is an excellent strategy for creating a foundation for living your best life.

References

Coleman, V.D. (2018). *Who am I? In H. Porter (Ed.), 40/40 Rules. Wisdom from 40 Women over 40, Volume II* (231-237). *Salt Lake City, Utah: Prosperity Publishing.*

Coleman, V.D. (2008). *A model of career development: 21st Century applications.* Australian Career Practitioner, Spring, 19, 19-20.

Coleman, V.D. (2005) 5 easy questions. *Unpublished manuscript. Las Vegas, Nevada.*

Coleman, V.D. & Barker, S.A. (1991). *Barriers to the career development of multicultural populations.* Educational and Vocational guidance, 52, 25-29.

Fitts, W. & Warren, W.L. (1996). Tennessee Self-Concept Scale 2nd Edition (TSCS-2). *Los CA: Western Psychological Services.*

Super, D.E., Starishevsky, R., Matlin, N., & Jordaan, J.P. (1963). Career development: Self-Concept theory. Essays in vocational development. *New York, New York: College Entrance Examination Board.*

Chapter Twenty-One

The Empowered Odyssey
By Niurka Coteron

Niurka Coteron is a distinguished growth strategist, transformation catalyst, and seasoned business mentor with over 30 years of notable career achievements. Excelling in executive leadership and global industry consulting across public, private, and non-profit sectors, she's left an enduring impact.

Author of *Begin From Within*, available on Amazon, Coteron shines as a luminary in her field. Her international speaking engagements captivate audiences with profound insights. She is recognized with esteemed accolades and showcases extensive business knowledge and dedication to empowering women to become millionaires.

As Founder and CEO of Insightful CFO, LLC, Coteron expertly leads professional accounting and management consulting. Her firm identifies and mends business gaps, optimizing operational excellence and profitability.

Additionally, as the visionary behind Unstoppable Being, LLC, Coteron empowers women through coaching, workshops, and digital courses, fostering confidence, leadership, and intentional life design.
www.linkedin.com/in/niurka-coteron-emba-cfo-cfe-cpa-a239025.

www.facebook.com/niurka.coteron

www.unstoppablebeing.com

The Empowered Odyssey

By Niurka Coteron

Arriving as an immigrant in a new country, armed with only a dream and unwavering determination, I embarked on a journey of transformation that would reshape my life and the lives of those around me. Despite the daunting challenges that awaited me, I clung to the belief in my inherent abilities and nurtured a burning desire to make a positive impact. Fueling my heart with determination and a commitment to service, I soon discovered the power within me to shape my destiny and live my best life.

My odyssey began in humility as I set foot on foreign soil, no friends, unfamiliar with the local language, climate, and culture . Yet, an unwavering conviction surged within me, a deep-seated belief that destiny had more in store for me.

Stripped of role models and refusing to be bound by the limitations of past generations, I challenged the feasibility of my extraordinary transformation. Though the idea appeared distant, the internal whispers gained volume, compelling me to leap into the unknown. Amidst the seeming chaos of that period in my life, an underlying certainty persisted, assuring me that more extraordinary things awaited.

The unyielding whisper, continuously affirming my destined greatness, transformed into an authentic call to action. It urged me to shun mediocrity and seize control of my circumstances, awakening my awareness of the latent potential within. Through the embrace of self-discovery, I grasped that change demanded the shedding of obsolete layers and embracing the new. Guided by curiosity and openness, I adapted to my evolving identity, navigating life's transitions with grace and resilience.

I embarked on a journey of understanding my values, passions, strengths, and vulnerabilities. Reflecting on my past experiences, I drew lessons from their impact on my present self. I humbly acknowledged areas where growth was required, fostering self-compassion. Embracing my unique identity, I liberated myself from the shackles of comparison, carving out an authentic life path. This realization that the core of my being was the bedrock of authenticity became my guiding light.

Beyond the clichés, living one's best life encapsulated a profound philosophy. It drove me to seize every fleeting moment and extract the utmost from my time on this wondrous planet. Anchored in self-understanding, purposeful goal setting, and the quest for fulfillment, this philosophy steered my journey.

As my self-awareness deepened, I penned meaningful goals aligned with my values and aspirations. I transcended conventional approaches by crafting a blend of short-term achievements and long-term ambitions. Occasionally, quantum leaps catapulted me forward, enabling me to focus on possibilities instead of being stifled by constraints.

However, success came hand in hand with its fair share of challenges. Maneuvering through the expansion of my business empire, I wrestled with the intricate balance between my professional endeavors and personal life. My determination to achieve equilibrium drove me forward, supported by the strength of my loving family.

Guided by an innate passion for aiding others, I ventured into various professional realms, delving into numbers and financial adventures. Yet, the persistent heart-whisper directed me toward my true vocation as a mentor and coach. Through mentoring, I harnessed my natural ability to empower entrepreneurs and business owners with financial acumen, helping them surmount obstacles and unleash their potential.

Recognizing the latent power within, I established my mentoring and coaching venture. Despite the shadow of doubt, the persistent whisper urged me to step into the light and share my expertise. It was time to unveil my talents, shedding the "best-kept secret" status.

My insatiable curiosity and hunger for knowledge led me to discover the optimal way to share my gifts. Months of unyielding research and perseverance bore fruit as I uncovered that pursuing my best life involved a holistic fusion of self-awareness, intention-setting, interpersonal connections, environmental harmony, daily rituals, nurturing, and compassion. Clear in my conviction, I recognized that cultivating emotional resilience, self-compassion, and embracing a growth mindset were pivotal in overcoming challenges and leading a life steeped in purpose and fulfillment.

As my insights grew more profound, I acquired a series of empowering acronyms that paved the way for a more balanced and enriched existence. One such acronym was E.N.L.I.G.H.T.E.N, an all-encompassing framework encapsulating nine fundamental components for embracing our optimal lives. This transformative journey underwent a deliberate division into three distinct phases: Illuminate, Empower, and Transform.

By embracing this framework, individuals equipped themselves with a comprehensive toolkit for self-discovery and personal develop-ment. Its all-encompassing approach paved the way for a more harmonious, purpose-driven, and fulfilling life, ultimately contributing to overall happiness and well-being.

I delved within the "Illuminate" phase, plumbing the depths of my passions, strengths, and aspirations. Guided meditations and introspection revealed my authentic desires, awakening a realiza-tion that I held the power to spark positive change, one step at a time.

Transitioning to the "Empower" phase, I focused on setting inten-tions and goals congruent with my newfound clarity. I learned to deconstruct grand visions into manageable steps, channeling my energies toward community improvement and creating avenues for prosperity.

With a solid foundation, the "Transform" phase beckoned, where I honed skills and nurtured resilience to surmount challenges. I paved my path toward transformation by navigating the terrain of leadership, fostering teamwork, and reframing challenges as stepping stones to growth.

As my journey through the Enlighten framework unfolded, the metamorphosis I underwent was palpable. Beyond professional accomplishments, the framework infused my personal life with vibrancy. I cultivated meaningful relationships, embraced mindfulness, and uncovered joy in the simple moments. Radiating positivity and kindness, I inspired others to embark on their quests of self-discovery.

Consequently, invitations to conferences arrived, urging me to share my experiences through the lens of the Enlighten framework. Humbly recounting my transformative journey, I underscored the significance of self-awareness, purpose-driven objectives, and unceasing personal growth.

My clients embarked on their journeys by immersing themselves in each framework component, reflecting on its relevance to their lives. This immersive 12-week program sought to instill a deep comprehension of the E.N.L.I.G.H.T.E.N. framework, arming participants with practical tools to surmount challenges and cultivate lives brimming with fulfillment and enlightenment. The course encompassed self-reflection, practical exercises, and the creation of actionable plans, ensuring that lasting positive change became an integral part of their lives.

Central to living our best lives is confronting challenging emotions with self-awareness, identifying triggers, employing coping mechanisms, and intertwining self-care and self-compassion into our existence. This approach, underpinned by the Enlighten framework, encapsulates a life imbued with purpose and meaning. It serves as a reminder that our journey toward empowerment is a testament to the strength of our resolve, the depth of our authenticity, and the ripples of transformation that extend far beyond our sphere.

Experiencing the joy of teaching my participants as they embark on their journey to live their best lives is truly an uplifting and fulfilling experience. Guiding individuals through a transformative process of self-discovery, growth, and empowerment allows me to witness their potential blossoming and realizing their dreams.

As a mentor and coach, I am a companion on their odyssey toward self-fulfillment. It is immensely gratifying to watch them embrace the framework's principles and witness their progress as they navigate the Illuminate, Empower, and Transform phases. A profound sense of satisfaction comes from seeing the impact of their dedication and hard work as they shed limiting beliefs and step into their authentic selves.

Each step of their journey brings a new opportunity for me to witness moments of realization, breakthroughs, and personal triumphs. The spark in their eyes when they uncover their passions and strengths during the Illuminate phase, the determination as they set meaningful goals during the Empower phase, and the resilience they exhibit as they tackle challenges and grow during the Transform phase—all these moments are a source of immense joy and inspiration.

The process of teaching and guiding participants as they embrace self-awareness, develop actionable plans, and cultivate positive habits resonates deeply with my passion for helping others unlock their potential. Seeing them transition from uncertainty to clarity, from self-doubt to empowerment, is a testament to the transformative power of self-discovery and intentional growth.

The joy of teaching lies in imparting knowledge and fostering a sense of community among participants. Witnessing them support and uplift each other, sharing their experiences, and celebrating their successes creates a positive and encouraging environment. This collaborative spirit adds an extra layer of fulfillment, knowing that the journey's impact extends beyond the individual to enrich the entire community's lives.

Ultimately, the joy in teaching participants to live their best lives stems from being a catalyst for positive change. Guiding them as they rewrite their narratives, overcome challenges, and embrace their authentic selves fills me with a sense of purpose and accomplishment.

Their journey becomes my journey, and their victories become my source of inspiration. It's a privilege to play a role in their transformation, witnessing them step into the fullness of their potential and live lives imbued with purpose, fulfillment, and joy. Through these actions and principles, I actively embody and embrace the essence of living my best life.

Chapter Twenty-Two

Embrace Your Red Door

By Rochelle Rondon

M eet Rochelle Rondon, an acclaimed marketing mastermind and an esteemed leader in the corporate world. As a highly sought-after Executive, Rochelle has been at the forefront of revolutionizing marketing strategies, driving exponential growth, and propelling businesses to unmatched success.

With an illustrious career spanning over two decades, Rochelle has consistently demonstrated an unparalleled ability to understand and navigate the ever-changing landscape of the business world. Her unyielding passion for marketing and her innate talent for identifying untapped potential have earned her a stellar reputation as a game-changer for companies seeking to elevate their brand presence.

As a true visionary, Rochelle possesses a unique insight into consumer behaviour, market trends, and cutting-edge technologies, allowing her to craft bespoke marketing blueprints tailored to each client's individual needs. She seamlessly blends innovation with tried-and-tested methodologies, empowering businesses to seize new opportunities and dominate their industries.

Rochelle has held senior roles at MySayToday, Chestnut Park Real Estate Limited, Fusion, and Operation Smile. Recognized by the Canadian Marketing Association and Data & Marketing Association for leading industry standards with data-driven and innovative strategies.

www.linkedin.com/in/ rochellerondon1

www.instagram.com/rochelle_rondon_

www.facebook.com/rondonway

www.rondonway.ca

Embrace Your Red Door

By Rochelle Rondon

Throughout my life, the mantra of dreaming big and never losing sight of my life's vision has been a guiding light.

The women who have graced my journey—my aunts and my mother—left an indelible mark on me. With their stunning big brown eyes, luxurious hair, impeccable makeup, and that iconic red Elizabeth Arden lipstick, they embodied elegance, grace, and strength.

As a young girl, I looked up to them, eagerly anticipating my 40s, where they seemed to have it all figured out. These incredible women of color knew how to savor life, embark on exciting adventures, whip up delectable meals, immerse themselves in movies and the theater, and soar in their careers.

As I contemplate the enigmatic smile of the Mona Lisa, I can't help but draw a connection between her timeless expression and the daily struggles I face as a woman. Balancing numerous roles—wife, mother, sister, daughter, friend, and now, as a woman in a leadership position—my life resembles a delicate juggling act. Some days, I feel overwhelmed, and tempted to throw in the towel. Others, I'm driven by an exhilarating surge of determination. The chatter of life often feels chaotic, fueled by coffee, my two joyful little girls, swayed by family commitments, and buried under endless piles of paperwork. But how do I navigate this beautiful chaos while staying true to myself?

～

In this chapter, I will share essential tips that have helped me embrace the journey of dreaming big and living my best life. By envisioning a life filled with joy and purpose, setting healthy boundaries to protect my well-being, surrounding myself with a supportive community, and nurturing self-care, I paint my life with vibrant hues of fulfillment and happiness.

Section 1: Embracing Your Vision

At the heart of living your best life lies the act of envisioning—a roadmap that propels you toward your aspirations and passions. The importance of defining your vision and staying committed to it is the key.

1.1 Discovering Your Passions and Goals

To build a vision that fuels your journey, you need to identify your passions and goals. Reflecting on what brings you joy and fulfillment allows you to set authentic and achievable targets that align with your true self.

1.2 Staying Committed to Your Vision

Life is a constantly shifting landscape, and your dreams may evolve as you grow. Staying committed to your vision requires adaptability and resilience. Embracing change allows you to seize new opportunities and shape your path accordingly.

1.3 Celebrating Milestones and Progress

Acknowledging your achievements and milestones along the way is vital. Celebrating progress fosters a sense of accomplishment, encourages you to keep pushing forward, and empowers you to overcome obstacles.

Section 2: Setting Boundaries for Empowerment

As a woman, it is easy to be stretched thin by the demands of others. It is a learned behavior that can be unlearned. Setting healthy boundaries to protect your well-being and maintain a sense of self is essential.

2.1 The Power of Saying No

Saying no is not an act of selfishness; it is an act of self-preservation. Learning to set boundaries empowers you to allocate your time and energy wisely, ensuring that you prioritize your needs alongside your responsibilities.

2.2 Cultivating Self-Advocacy

Advocating for yourself, your thoughts, and your ideas is essential in both personal and professional settings. Building confidence in self-expression will strengthen your voice and enhance your impact.

2.3 Recognizing and Addressing Guilt

As a woman, guilt can often accompany my choices to prioritize self-care. Be kind to yourself and recognize and address guilt, allowing you to embrace self-care without reservation.

Section 3: Building a Supportive Community

No woman is an island; cultivating meaningful connections with others enriches your life and nurtures personal growth in a way that helps you be surrounded by a diverse community of people which is a supportive network.

3.1 The Power of Sisterhood

The bonds formed with other women can be transformative. Embracing sisterhood allows you to learn how to uplift and inspire others, creating a community of support and encouragement.

3.2 Embracing Mentorship and Learning

Seeking mentorship and being open to continuous learning broadens your horizons and enriches your perspectives. These relationships provide guidance, inspiration, and opportunities for both professional and personal growth.

3.3 Embracing Diversity in Relationships

Welcoming diversity in your social circles exposes you to a multitude of perspectives, cultures, and experiences. Connecting with individuals from different backgrounds fosters inclusivity and nurtures your personal growth.

Section 4: Nurturing Self-Care and Well-Being

To thrive on your journey, you must prioritize self-care and well-being. You have to nurture your physical, mental, and emotional health.

4.1 Mindfulness and Meditation

Incorporating mindfulness and meditation into your daily routine promotes inner peace and emotional resilience. These practices allow you to stay present, manage stress, and find solace in moments of chaos.

4.2 Embracing Creativity and Passion Projects

Indulging in creative pursuits will unleash the inner artist and allow you to express yourself authentically. Whether it's through art, writing, dance, or any other form of creativity, embracing passion projects nourishes your soul.

4.3 The Importance of Rest and Reflection

In the pursuit of your dreams, you must not neglect rest and reflection. Taking moments of solitude to recharge and assess your progress aids in maintaining balance and a positive outlook.

Embracing your vision, setting healthy boundaries, cultivating a supportive community, and nurturing self-care from the essence of living your best life. As you dream big and strive for your own aspirations, I choose to paint my life with vivid hues, leaving behind a beautiful masterpiece. Through resilience, empowerment, and authentic self-expression, I have crafted a life that truly reflects who I am and what brings me joy. So, embrace the journey of dreaming big in red lipstick, empower to transform your life, and uplift those around you.

Chapter Twenty-Three

My Journey to Becoming a SHERO
By Pearl Chiarenza

Pearl Chiarenza is a Mental Fitness Life Coach, Author, and Speaker. She loves helping women put themselves first without guilt, empowering them to overcome being a people pleaser as they become SHEROs of their lives.

She never thought she would say that her son Matt was now an Angel who they lost in July of 2022. Her chapter is an inspiration and dedicated to Matt. Why? – because he used to say, "Mom, no matter what gets in your way or how someone mistreats you, I can't get over how you see the glass half full." She always responded that her glass is not half full – it's overflowing! Losing Matt was hard. She pushed through because she never could see the glass half empty when her husband of 35 years, Chuck and her sons Matt and Nate brought much joy and happiness along the way.

www.linkedin.com/in/pearl-chiarenza-8269a8b
www.instagram.com/pearl_chiarenza
www.facebook.com/pearlchiarenza
www.wsliving.com/
www.wslivingretreats.com

My Journey to Becoming a SHERO

By Pearl Chiarenza

I want to share my personal journey of transformation from a people pleaser to a SHERO. My life has been a rollercoaster of self-discovery, growth, and empowerment.

Years ago, my introduction would have focused on being a wife, a mom, and all the roles I played for others. I found it challenging to say "No" and put myself first because I feared it would upset people or make them think I did not care about them. The word "Yes" came easily to me, but it often left me feeling drained and disconnected from my true self.

I knew deep down that I needed to change. Putting myself first didn't mean being selfish; it meant recognizing my worth and honoring my needs. The journey to embracing my best life began with overcoming my people-pleasing tendencies.

I had always been a giver, a nurturer, and someone who wanted to make everyone happy. But in the process of doing so, I lost sight of my own desires, dreams, and aspirations. It was as if I had become a shadow of myself, living my life based on the expectations and demands of others.

∾

One day, as I looked in the mirror, I hardly recognized the person staring back at me. That was the moment I knew I had to make a change. I couldn't continue living a life that was not my own.

Learning to say "No" was a daunting task, but I was determined to break free from the cycle of constantly sacrificing my own desires. It required setting boundaries and learning to prioritize my well-being without feeling guilty.

Trust me, it wasn't like this happened overnight! The guilt I had in saying "No" was the hardest thing to overcome and took me a few months to really step into the confidence that mattered, and I had to show up first in my life!

As I started to say "No" to things that didn't align with my joy and purpose, something remarkable happened. I started to notice the doors it opened for others. When I declined opportunities I couldn't fully commit to, I created space for someone else to step in and shine. I became known as a connector, empowering those around me to embrace their own potential.

With each "No" I confidently expressed; I felt a newfound strength within me. I felt happier, more empowered, and radiant. It was as if I had rediscovered the essence of who I truly was. Stepping into the power of "No" allowed me to show up fully for my business, my family, and my friends. It was a journey of self-liberation that brought me closer to living my best life.

Breaking free from people-pleasing also led me to realize that many women shared similar struggles. The pressure to always put others first seemed to be a common thread among us. I wanted to help other women break free from this cycle and embrace their own power.

This realization inspired me to create a space where women could be empowered to become the SHERO they are by being Stronger, Happier, Empowered, Radiant and Original women waiting to make their mark on their dreams and visions without guilt. This is where my SHERO Method was born! A 4-month program, a transformative 4-month roadmap designed to guide women on their journey to a fulfilled life. Through the program, I teach women to prioritize self-care, break unhealthy habits, and communicate their needs confidently.

The SHERO Method is not just a set of tools or techniques; it is a mindset shift that empowers women to step into their authentic selves. It is about embracing our uniqueness, strengths, and vulnerabilities and using them as sources of power and growth.

One of the most significant shifts occurred when we lost our beloved son, Matthew, at the age of 25 in 2022. His passing was devastating, but it reinforced the importance of living life to the fullest. I found strength in living as a SHERO, honoring his memory, and continuing to pursue my dreams.

People often remark on my strength and resilience, not understanding how I manage to carry on with such determination. I tell them that it is because I embrace the SHERO within me. That I had to continue living, no longer feeling guilty about putting myself first, because I know it allows me to be the best version of myself for those I love, and I would not be honoring Matt's memory if I lived differently after his passing.

Through my journey I realized the struggle I had was with voicing my needs to my family, friends, and clients. Learning to communicate my realistic expectations, I was able to confidently share my personal needs, desires, and expectations with my family, friends, and colleagues. I discovered that open and honest communication was bringing me deeper connections and allowing others to know the real me.

Today, I walk through life with a sense of purpose and meaning. I wake up each morning excited for the day ahead, energized by the beauty of the world, and empowered to face any challenges with a positive mindset. Trust me, I still miss my son every day, and I have faith that, if I continue to show up as my own SHERO, all will create my best life.

The journey to becoming a SHERO has been a transformative one, filled with growth, self-empowerment, and authenticity. It's my mission to inspire other women to embrace their power, break free from people-pleasing, and step into their greatness.

One of the things I love to do is share the principles and practices that I learned in the creation of the SHERO Method, not as a sales pitch, but as a heartfelt invitation to join me on a journey of self-discovery and empowerment. Together, I help women unlock their potential within and create a life that brings them joy, fulfillment, and the courage to embrace our inner pearls of greatness. Supporting each other to become the SHEROs of their lives, shining brightly and inspiring others to do the same brings me a beautiful sense of joy.

As we navigate the challenges and triumphs of life, I want to remind you that you, too, have the power to embrace your inner SHERO. We need to remember: it's not about being perfect or having it all figured out, but about owning your story, vulnerabilities, and strengths. When you live authentically and prioritize your well-being, you become an unstoppable force, radiating positive energy to everyone around you.

But before embarking on this transformative adventure, let's explore the power of forging a great mindset. One of the things that helped me is learning to meditate. I was not someone who did your typical meditations; I reached out to a friend Sharon RG with Mending Meditation who specially designed meditations to help me release unwanted thoughts, stress, and fear that were brewing in the background of my mind. Picture yourself taking one hour a day to create a sense of peace, allowing you to anchor the present moment and boost your awareness of what's happening internally from a mental, physical, and emotional point of view. Through these empowering meditations, I was able to let go of what no longer served me and find calm amidst chaos and overwhelm.

In addition to commanding your mind, my new SHERO Cape allowed me to take back control of my body. Discovering my super-powers of self-discipline as I created self-care habits for sleeping, hydration, and nutrition. When I applied the SHERO Method mind-set, I was able to see my life as a series of choices, where you are constantly in control of your life and destiny. Your body becomes a temple of strength and vitality, supporting you on your journey to becoming the best version of yourself.

The path to embracing your inner SHERO is an all-encompassing one, where mind, body, and soul work are in harmony. As I delved into the intricacies of becoming a SHERO, I was able to uncover how each element contributes to your transformation and empowerment. I love helping women now embark on this transformative journey, supporting and uplifting each other as we embrace the power within and uncover the brilliance of our inner pearls of greatness. As SHEROs, we have the strength, the wisdom, and the courage to live our best lives and inspire others to do the same. I love to and want you to shine brightly and create a ripple effect of empowerment, spreading positivity and radiance to every corner of the world.

I believe we all come into this world and, as our journey unfolds, each of us is like an oyster, rough on the outside but harboring an inner pearl of greatness. Becoming a SHERO is about tapping into that inner pearl, embracing our uniqueness, and living life authentically.

Chapter Twenty-Four

Unstuck: You Can Reframe Your Life
By Dr. Oyindamola Okenla

D r. Oyindamola Okenla is a transformational life and mental health coach, counselor, and award-winning author. A certified John Maxwell coach, speaker, and trainer, she is also a serial entrepreneur and prophetic intercessor. Dr. Damola holds a doctorate in mental health counseling. With over 15 years of experience, she has counseled and coached her clients, guiding them through relationship and marital trauma to achieve better mental health.

Her extensive experience and Ph.D. research have led her to

develop a unique framework for empowering women to overcome challenges, transforming them from feeling defeated and depressed to restored and renewed. Dr. Okenla is dedicated to helping women reach their godly potential, using their pain and possibilities for power, purpose, to make impact, and profit. Her approach combines expertise and real-life experience to effectively serve her clients. Her profound faith identity guides her mission to make a positive impact on others' lives.

www.linkedin.com/in/dr-damola-okenla-7ba26353
www.instagram.com/coachdto
www.facebook.com/CoachDTO
www.damolatreasureokenla.com

UNSTUCK: You Can Reframe Your Life

By Dr. Oyindamola Okenla

We carry previous pains and traumas through life. These events can hinder us from living our best lives. Reframing our stories and finding healing strength can empower others to do the same. My transformation and resilience may motivate another woman to live her best life.

Life throws us strange challenges that can haunt us. Trauma and pain leave us in a circle of regret and sorrow. With resilience and determination, you can overcome the past and embrace a joyful and fulfilling future. In this chapter, I will talk about overcoming trauma, rethinking my life, and finding my best life. I hope it inspires other women to find solace, healing, and empowerment to live their best lives.

Healing from the Past

I started by admitting I could not ignore my past. My recovery, transformation, and best life began there. If you want the best life as a woman, you must acknowledge the past, assess it, and reevaluate it. It is important not to judge or criticize yourself. Instead, please take what you've learned and apply it. Keep in mind that yesterday was yesterday.

Facing our ghosts and accepting their influence takes courage. Therapy, support groups, and reflective thinking can help us overcome the pain and heal.

Embracing the Power of Self-Care

Self-care transformed my life. Healing requires self-care. Emotional health affects mental and physical health. I learned self-compassion via joyful and peaceful pursuits. Hobbies like meditation, journaling, writing, prayer, and worship may transform. Self-care is essential to personal progress; it is not selfish.

Setting Boundaries and Embracing Empowerment

Learning to create healthy boundaries to live your best life is critical. This includes saying no to toxic relationships, surroundings, and events that no longer serve you. Accept your authority and restore your individuality and originality.

Surround yourself with people who encourage and support you and take part in activities that reflect your core values and interests. You cannot revisit the same people or locations that hurt you and expect to be whole.

Seeking Support and Building Community

Recovery and transformation require others. I learned to seek help from dependable friends, family, and experts. I found comfort, affirmation, and encouragement in kind people. I found a network of women with comparable tragedies by sharing my tales, which empowered me. Three of my books came from inspirations from my meet-ups. Share your stories and help others to unburden and live their best life and you are sure to have yours.

Reframing the Narrative

Reframing past traumas could help with recovery. My pain enabled me to evolve and change. I discovered my strength and tenacity by changing my perspective rather than becoming a victim. I triumphed, rewriting my story one more time.

The Power of Forgiveness and Resilience

You must forgive to live your best life.

Forgiveness is not about condoning or ignoring the harm perpetrated on us but about releasing the emotional baggage that holds us bound to the past. For my freedom and wholeness, I learned to forgive. By forgiving myself and those who hurt me, I restored my power.

Personal progress depends on resilience. Resilience is not just bouncing back from trauma and pain but harnessing the suffering to grow.

Resilience helped me turn tragedy into wisdom and confront future obstacles with confidence, commitment, and self-worth. Challenges help you progress on your recovery path. You may build resilience by practicing mindfulness, coping mechanisms, and emotional well-being.

Remember, you are stronger than you believe!

Crafting a Vision for the Future

Healing opens up future possibilities. I created a vision for my ideal life with clarity and purpose, embracing my newfound power and resilience. I found fulfillment in my business and ministry by setting realistic goals.

As an everyday woman who wants to live her best life, you must prioritize your serenity and happiness and trust yourself to make decisions aligned with your authentic self.

Rediscovering Passions and Purpose

In my pursuit of healing and living my best life, I embarked on a journey of self-discovery, I reconnected with my passions, exploring activities that brought me joy and a sense of fulfillment. In the process, I discovered my purpose-to inspire and uplift other women who had experienced similar pain and trauma.

By aligning my life with this goal, I found a renewed sense of meaning and empowerment. No matter how messy it has been, always go back to ask yourself why. That will inspire the rediscovery of passion and purpose. Connect with the activities that bring you a sense of fulfillment. By aligning your life with your values and passions, you unlock a profound sense of purpose and joy.

Holistic Healing for Personal Growth

Mental, emotional, and physical healing are interconnected. Holistic recovery was essential to me, so I tried different strategies. I gained resilience and self-compassion via counseling, prayers, and inner healing coaching.

Reframing My Mindset

Reframing my thinking was one of the most significant changes I made. I stopped seeing my history as failures and started seeing them as opportunities. This transformation helped me to realize the power and wisdom I had earned through conquering tough times. I set the stage for personal growth by questioning negative thought patterns and adopting self-affirming attitudes. I learned not to let my past define me by telling myself it's merely a portion of my existence. I started talking to myself positively, promoting self-love and kindness.

Paying it Forward

As I experienced my transformation, I felt a deep calling to uplift and empower other women who had faced similar challenges. I became an advocate for change, using my voice and experiences to create awareness and support others on their healing journeys. My experience even became the basis for my dissertation on intimate partner violence.

Through mentoring, volunteering or even starting an organization, you can harness your strength and uplift those around you.

Living in the Present Moment

While remembering the past and planning for the future are vital, it's crucial to live in the now. Appreciate and celebrate tiny and big accomplishments in the present. Being present helps us to appreciate life's beauty and progress.

Dr. Sarah Thompson, a renowned psychologist and women's empowerment coach, emphasizes the importance of self-discovery and healing for women on their journey to living their best lives. She asserts,

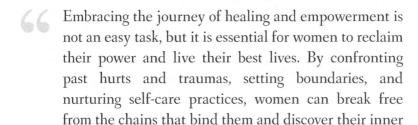 Embracing the journey of healing and empowerment is not an easy task, but it is essential for women to reclaim their power and live their best lives. By confronting past hurts and traumas, setting boundaries, and nurturing self-care practices, women can break free from the chains that bind them and discover their inner strength.

The journey to empowerment is a transformative one, leading to a sense of purpose, resilience, and joy. It is my hope that this chapter will inspire women to embark on their paths of healing and empowerment, knowing that they are not alone on this journey."

Lessons for Other Women: *Takeaways*

I want to share my life lessons with other ladies who want to live their best lives:

1. Acknowledge your pain: Embrace your unpleasant history to heal and evolve. Accept that you're wounded, but don't let it define you.
2. Seek support: Surround yourself with understanding friends, therapists, and support groups. Healing flourishes in a supportive community.
3. Reframe your narrative: Challenge the victimization attitude and focus on your talents, resilience, and insight from prior experiences. You've triumphed.
4. Practice self-compassion and forgiveness: Understanding that recovery is a journey and setbacks are normal, be compassionate to yourself. Release animosity through forgiving yourself and others.
5. Engage in activities that bring you joy and align your life with meaning and fulfillment: Embracing your passions can lead you to your purpose and ignite a sense of purposeful living.
6. Build a supportive community: Share your journey, uplift others, and create safe spaces where women can heal and thrive together. Together, we can build a network of empowerment and encouragement.

As we close this chapter, I encourage you to act. It's time to start living your best life with your newfound knowledge. Put the tips above into practice and discover how it transforms your life.

Begin today. Set significant goals, reflect on your self-awareness, and find opportunities for growth and transformation. Change and push yourself. Affirm your value and appreciate the riches around you. Appreciate every moment's beauty.

Living your best life is achievable. I suggest the following: Apply these ideas to your daily life. Seek out more resources, engage with like-minded people, and keep learning.

Remember, you can build the best life you want. Take this chance to explore yourself and find happiness. It's yours to have.

In the words of Naeem Callaway, "Sometimes the smallest step in the right direction ends up being the biggest step of your life. Tiptoe if you must but take the step." Healing, empowerment, and living unstuck will turn your life into one of purpose, pleasure, and fulfillment. Let us lift each other and inspire the world with our resilience and success. Best yet!

Chapter Twenty-Five

Embracing Our Spiritual Journey
By Dr. Eileen McDowell

D r. Eileen McDowell is a PhD, LPC, MBA, CHypno, Licensed RTT Therapist.

She has been drawn to the arts, writing, music and why people "do what they do" since she was a little girl. She has always been a strong empath and known most of her life that she had a superpower: to help people heal. Not the doctor/surgery/"say ah" kind of healing. The emotional healer in her drove her ambitions to empower others to achieve whatever they desire. She helps others discover, reach, and exceed their goals both professionally and personally.

We all suffer tragedy, are presented with obstacles to overcome and are challenged to pick ourselves up off the ground at some point in our life. This is the sounding board for growth and necessary when we lack presence. There are messages in our experiences that provide the path to our life mission. When we listen to the silence, God, Source and the Universe provides us with answers.

The power of the mind is fascinating, mysterious and magical. Studies have unveiled amazing discoveries in the past 10 years regarding the endless possibilities of neuroplasticity, the suggestibility of the conscious vs subconscious and energy frequencies. Through her life journey, experiences and extensive studies, it became her mission to share the amazing power we have to naturally heal ourselves and accelerate our divine infinite potential.

www.linkedin.com/in/eileenmcdowell

www.instagram.com/hypnolife365

www.facebook.com/HypnoLife365

www.hypnolife365.com

Embracing Our Spiritual Journey

By Dr. Eileen McDowell

Buckle in ladies, because this could potentially be the most valuable advice you'll ever hear... It changed my life.

In our fast-paced digital world, it is easy to become consumed by the demands and expectations of success and what others need and think. As innately nurturing women, we neglect our own needs, desires, and the unique path that calls to us, failing to pay attention to our own well-being and personal alignment which can lead to wasted time and unnecessary suffering. I'm going to give you the fastest way to bliss.

I grew up in Bel Air, Los Angeles where Hollywood rules all. Who I knew was more important than who I was. From a very young age, I learned to care more about what others thought of me than what I thought of myself. It felt isolating, like I never was or ever could be enough. Now, with social media ruling the world, I believe most of the population feels the way I felt growing up. I graduated from Marymount High School, and still today it's known as the high school the Kardashians went to rather than one of the most prestigious all girls college-prep high schools in Los Angeles county. Hollywood influence at its best.

By the time I graduated I had zero clue who I was, what inspired me or what blew my socks off. All I was clear on was that I didn't feel like I was enough and sought out the easiest attention I could receive... from men. As a beautiful, highly educated teen on my way to undergrad on scholarship, I felt 2 feet tall and inadequate in every way. Why? From an outsider looking in, I had everything; I was everything that so many wanted to be. I felt tiny in my world because I lacked the most important concept most are unaware of: self-alignment.

Self-alignment holds immense significance in our lives, enabling us to discover our true purpose, find fulfillment, and navigate the challenges that come our way, no matter how difficult. At the core of self-alignment lies the understanding that each individual possesses a distinct set of values, beliefs, and aspirations. These factors, combined with our unique talents and passions, form the essence of our being where bliss is found. Did you catch that part? Read the last two sentences again. Underline them and commit them to memory, Ladies!! I promise, it will not steer you wrong.

When we disregard or suppress these intrinsic aspects of ourselves, we become disconnected from our authentic Self. Then guess what happens? We may find ourselves pursuing paths that are incongruent with our true nature, leading to a sense of dissatisfaction and internal conflict. What does that look like? For me, it was wasting my time dating men who treated me the way I felt about myself, marrying an alcoholic who terrorized me and my 7 year old son. Spending time in partial hospitalization with severe complex relational PTSD. Having to start my career over again several times in my life. When we lack self alignment, the universe, God, Source (whatever your belief system is) will slam you down and make the house of cards fall so that you can build the story you were destined to have. This fall is usually difficult, painful, stressful, exhausting and ultra challenging. Let me save you a lot of grief. Get aligned first, then step forward.

Most measure success solely by external standards such as wealth, social status, or material possessions. However, true success lies in aligning our actions with our inner purpose, not conforming to external expectations. Embracing self-alignment allows us to prioritize our own needs and desires, making conscious choices that reflect our values and bring us closer to a sense of fulfillment. There's that bliss again. Doesn't living in bliss sound heavenly? I can tell you from experience that it is very difficult to get there when you live to please everyone else. It didn't matter how many degrees I had (and I have a lot), how much money I made or how successful my businesses were; I kept choosing the wrong men, building the businesses that were boring to me, feeling miserable, aged, drained, physically unhealthy and lost, exhausting myself as I ran on the hamster wheel of misalignment, getting nowhere.

It wasn't until I let go of what everyone else thought of me, caring about what everyone else needed from me and giving up my energy to others who gladly sucked me dry, that I discovered that true wealth begins inside myself.

Neglecting our personal alignment can result in so much wasted time/life as we find ourselves caught up in endeavors that do not serve our higher purpose. It is easy to get swept away by societal pressures, familial expectations, or the desire to please others. However, the longer we persist on a path misaligned with our true selves, the more time we squander, leaving us feeling unfulfilled and unworthy.

Furthermore, ignoring our own needs and desires can lead to emotional and spiritual pain, experiencing a sense of emptiness, restlessness, or even depression when we deny the unique essence of who we are. Our true selves are intricately connected to our spiritual well-being and, by neglecting this aspect, we risk losing touch with our inner guidance and the wisdom that resides within.

So what can you do next? To embark on a journey of self-alignment, it is crucial to cultivate self-awareness and introspection. Taking time for introspection allows us to reflect on our values, passions, and aspirations. So how do you do that? Listening to the whispers of your soul and discovering what truly brings you joy and meaning.

Here are some practices that I give everyone of my clients and practice myself on a daily basis. Meditation, journaling, spending time in nature, walking, listening to music, getting into water, leaving your phone at home, disconnecting from electronics, laughing, getting rid of the toxic people in your life. These are just a few suggestions to create space for self-reflection which enables us to connect with our deepest selves, our true Self, and gain clarity on our true path to ultimate happiness. Seek guidance from spiritual mentors, participate in workshops, or join supportive communities. Seek out those who can provide valuable insights and encouragement along your journey. I personally have spent hundreds of thousands of dollars in education and mentoring which does not include two masters degrees, certifications and a doctorate. Yes, I embrace my Nerd Self too! Suround yourselves with like-minded individuals who understand the importance of self-alignment. When I chose me, I practiced daily spiritual and growth routines, took care of my body, mind and spirit and chose to put myself first, my life made an extraordinary trajectory toward deep happiness and satisfaction.

Look, I've been through the mill. I lost my husband to cancer when my son was nine months old, was hospitalized for severe post traumatic stress disorder, married an alcoholic ignoring all the signs thinking I could handle it... the list goes on. I can tell you in all of the shitty experiences that I have had in my life I was focused on what everybody else needed, what everybody else wanted and what made everybody else happy. Meanwhile, I was miserable inside. One day when I was in PHP for PTSD, I parked for my daily visit, and the most beautiful feather I have ever seen gently fell onto the hood of my car, slowly spiraling down. As I watched it, I had an undeniable calming feeling come across me. Somehow I knew in that moment that I wasn't alone, and that I needed to release resistance and ask for help.

When I did that, I started to focus on myself and the things that I needed and let go of what the entire world thought of me. Fast forward to today. I have a thriving business helping women not only align themselves with who they are but love themselves unconditionally, treat their body with respect and give energetic output that brings in the same beautiful energy back into their lives, transitioning to mind, body, and soul wellness.

I figured out how to do this the hard, rough and tumble way. I want to save you the rough and tumble route. Not everybody has to experience the traumatic journey that I experienced but most of us are stubborn, live from ego and think we know better. Trust me, you don't and we are all learning every day. When you let go and self alignment, everything falls into place. Use this chapter to shorten your path to bliss. Focus on yourself, your needs and things that you want. This is not selfish, it is simply necessary. When you do this, your energetic vibration will rise, and you will attract exactly what it is that you were meant to have and meant to be.

All My Love, Dr. Eileen McDowell.

Chapter Twenty-Six

The Dirty "R" Word
By Leah Rodriquez DeSalles

L eah Rodriquez DeSalles is an Author, Speaker, and Strategy Pro. She is a visionary best known for advocating biblical rest and an outstanding ability to construct systems of ideas. Leah has traveled, spoken, and coached in India, Japan, Ukraine, Mexico, the Netherlands, Canada, France, and at the University of the Nations in Kona, Hawaii, to international students worldwide.

Leah is the founder of Armed Ambassadors, an equipping entity. She is known internationally for her blog, Grapplings, and Christian Fiction Novels.

With over 35 years of Award-Winning Business Performance, Leah developed Emphasis on Integrity, a program officially recognized as an Expert System with qualifications in strategy planning and recovery.

Please visit **leahdesalles.com** to download her free e-book, *Emphasis on Integrity: The Solution to Burnout.*

Short, vocal, and fiercely loyal, Leah lives in Arizona with her husband, Rudy, and their dogs, Dash and Dot.

www.linkedin.com/in/leahdesalles

www.instagram.com/armedambassadors

www.facebook.com/LeahDeSalles

www.leahdesalles.com

The Dirty "R" Word

By Leah Rodriquez DeSalles

Well, hello! Who is this chick? Why should I listen to her?

Hi. I'm Leah, and I used to struggle with self-neglect. Today, I walk in a manner worthy of the call on my life while exercising the self-care required for quality performance. I am the Founder of Armed Ambassadors, which equips individuals who have pushed too hard for too long and don't know how to stop.

Oh, hello.

It's an honor to have achieved personal and professional goals I never dreamed possible. But what some people don't realize is that I'm not that special. I don't have any letters behind my name, and like many, I come from a broken home where we lived below the poverty level. Neither of my parents went to college, and they certainly didn't encourage me to. We were blue-collar workers, and the message was sent to us that *you work hard all day, every day, 40-plus hours a week until you die.* And sometimes, you get a vacation. A union job was hitting the jackpot, and I did all that.

The only problem was that no one told me that having a Spirit of Excellence didn't mean I had to kill myself. So, believing that my job was my identity and that if I wasn't producing, I wasn't a valid human being... I worked, worked, and worked some more until the line between my personal and professional life barely existed. I poured every ounce of my being into everything I did until, not once... but twice, I suffered a debilitating health crash that left me broken down and even bedridden.

What did I learn? That to live my best life, I seriously needed to exercise the art of rest. Yes, *rest.* The dirty R word.

Some of you just breathed a sigh of relief because someone is actually going to give you permission to rest, and I just lost many because resting isn't a realistic option for you.

Look, I've overcome some difficult things, came out on the other side successfully, and I want to give you the benefit of what I've learned. While you need to know how to radically shift your Return on Investment (ROI) in life.

But I promise that before we are done, I'll show you where you can go to get more information on this. Today, I want to give you the most valuable keys to get you started. So, I will share the three most important things you can do right now to achieve life-changing results!

No, really.

First, Clarity. The crucial first step in achieving proper rest that allows you to perform better and be an all-around healthier person... is clarity. One of my favorite questions is, "What am I responsible for, and what am I NOT responsible for?" Clarifying what you want, need, and must do can help determine your perspective on how to move forward and get off the rat wheel! Once you separate the lies (what you've been telling yourself) and the truth (what is absolutely required), you'll be able to strategize a plan of action that permits rest and empowers your success.

Next, you need to exercise the power of The Guilt-Free No. Want to know the three no-fail keys to gaining peace of mind?

- Boundaries
- Boundaries
- Boundaries

You may think you know about boundaries, but you must do more than know about them; you must utilize them for success and freedom. Once you begin drawing hard lines, you will understand and implement how to regain control along with your treasured peace.

Let's remember that we honestly can't control everything (as much as we'd like to), but we can control some things, and that is where the beauty of boundaries comes in. What we can't control, we surrender to the One who can.

Finally, Find Your Fills. (What fills your tank?)

Do you want the blueprint that will eliminate imbalance forever? Here it is: Rest and Stress Management. Sounds too simple? It's not. When you learn the indispensable elements needed to restore and refuel, you'll find the pathway to peace that will serve you for a lifetime.

After my first health crash, I watched a pastor with a message that changed my life. I went into my bathroom and wept on the floor in a ball of snot. I thought I was losing my mind but, as I learned, I was simply running on empty. Perfectly clearly, I heard the Lord say, "Now you know. Don't do it again." I wish I could say I learned to rest and never found myself crashing again... but I didn't.

The not-so-fun truth in life is that until we learn a lesson well, we will face it again and again until we get it right. I was great at taking care of myself for a while, but in good ol' type-A fashion, I jumped right back into my pattern of push and ended up in bed debilitated... again. What took four years to recover from the first time only took two years the second time, and I have been exercising the Guilt-Free No and Finding my Fills ever since.

What is Finding Your Fill? It's discovering the things in life that fulfill you. Not what the girls are doing and insisting you join, not what family members enjoy, not what you think you should enjoy because... no. What do YOU enjoy? What calms you down and satisfies you? The sad truth is that many of us work so hard to please others and check all the boxes that we may not even know what fills our tank!

I remember seeing a picture on a friend's wall that said something about 'Your Dreams Coming True.' I was so disturbed. I realized, *I don't even know what my dreams are anymore.* No wonder I had two crashes! I had nothing that filled my tank or goals to reach for! I was just trying to survive.

Some examples of what fills your tank may be: Crocheting,

gardening, listening to music, dancing, running, swimming, praying, meditation, you name it. I have a girlfriend who loves watching Japanese movies to unwind. Why? She's not sure! It's just what works for her!

You are never trapped; there are so many apps and avenues to help you relax and unwind. You just have to find your thang. Which ones do I like? The One Minute Pause App by Wild at Heart. LOVE IT. Also, Lectio 365. So good! When was the last time you read a book... for fun? (Giiiirl, I hope you're having fun now! But you know what I mean.)

Does all of this make sense? Is some of it hitting a bit close to home? Good! Coming out of denial is the first step! Revelation is key. As Dr. Maya Angelou said, "When we know better, we do better."

So, now you know.

Look, we'd all love some balance in life, but the truth is that we rarely get it. Instead of focusing on the ever-eluding balance, why don't we seek those areas of our lives that require emphasis in different seasons? This season it may be your health or children. Last season it was your mother or sister. Your husband, job, education... Where is your emphasis required this season? Where is your focus? How can we accomplish these things well while maintaining our sanity and still gaining peace of mind? By placing our *Emphasis on Integrity*.

As promised, I'd love to share where you can go to get more information on these truths and more! Please visit my website, leahdesalles.com, and download my free e-book, *Emphasis on Integrity; The Solution to Burnout*. This little book will guide you to additional tools for learning to have an Emphasis on Integrity while gaining crucial clarity, drawing hard lines, getting proper rest, and managing your stress.

In the meantime, what are two action steps you can take immediately?

1. **Kick Fear and Anxiety in the Rear:** When you face your fears, start asking yourself the right clarifying questions, and identify your limiting core beliefs. Peace of mind is right around the corner.
2. **Get Help:** No man is an island; you weren't created to white-knuckle it. Embrace the Biblical Strategies for Success. "Whatever you hold in your mind on a consistent basis is exactly what you will experience in your life." - Tony Robbins.

You are not alone, and you are worth the effort. If this book is in your hands, I've already prayed for you. So, let's do this!

Chapter Twenty-Seven

My Journey from Self-Loathing to Self-Love
By Dr. Laura Kaspar

D r. Laura Kaspar has been self-employed her entire adult life having successfully managed and owned businesses from Los Angeles to New York. None have been more fulfilling than the career she has today as a PHD, Certified Clinical Hypnotherapist. She has been incredibly fortunate to grow this business alongside her twin sister, Eileen McDowell. With individual talents, together they make one dynamic team.

She has had incredible wins like building a million-dollar-a-year real estate company to crushing losses including embezzlement leading to bankruptcy, an illness that nearly took her life, and a painful unexpected divorce. Her most profound lesson: by releasing traumas and fears using hypnosis, she was able to quickly move forward in the most healthy, happy and abundant way possible and she has never been happier!

Pain is a part of our life's journey and we can choose whether it makes or breaks us. What defines us is how we learn from our experiences and grow into something that is even more powerful than before.

She finds it tremendously rewarding to be able to help her clients overcome their own adversities. Magic is inside all of us. She pulls personal power out of her clients, quickly clearing the blocks that hold them back, reprograming their minds for success and watching them shine!

www.linkedin.com/in/laura-kaspar-hypnolife

www.instagram.com/explore/tags/thekaspartwins

www.instagram.com/Hypnolife365

www.facebook.com/HypnoLife365

Instagram.com/Hypnolife365

www.hypnolife365.com

My Journey from Self-Loathing to Self-Love

By Dr. Laura Kaspar

For a decade, I wore weight gain and depression like an ill-fitting suit, an unforgiving cloth that clung to every part of me. My mirror reflection morphed into a cruel parody, and my body became a monument to self-loathing. My mind, once a haven, turned into a battleground littered with shards of self-esteem and fragments of confidence.

I carried the excess weight, both physical and emotional, like chains, shackling me in my daily life. Every glance in the mirror, every struggle to fit into clothes, and every unsolicited piece of advice a harsh reminder of my ongoing battle. I worked obsessively, perhaps to drown out the misery and distract myself from the pain of existence. But the more I worked, the heavier my chains grew.

A parade of bad relationships trod through my life, each one leaving me more broken and disillusioned. The hurt accumulated, the pain, the betrayal. I allowed it to pull me down into an abyss of despair.

I was sick and tired, not just of the way I looked but of the way I felt. I yearned for change; I longed for liberation from my own body and from my own mind. Driven by desperation and a burning desire for change, I decided to take drastic measures to shed the weight that had become my identity and my prison. The decision was not easy, nor was the path that lay ahead. But it was necessary for my physical health, for my mental well-being, for my very survival.

I made the unorthodox choice to have elective gastric sleeve surgery. Not here in the United States. The cost was unaffordable for elective surgery, and I was not "sick" enough to qualify for the coverage. To qualify, I needed to have three or more deadly ailments like Type 2 diabetes, severe sleep apnea, heart disease, high blood pressure, or a body mass index of over 35. It was clear I was well on my way to all of these ailments I was trying to avoid. Why would I wait?

I found a hospital in Tijuana whose cost was a third of that in the US. It was a leap of faith. I had done my research. The hospital, though touted as state-of-the-art, was worlds apart from its American counterparts. It gleamed under the Mexican sun, floors shining, instruments sparkling, an extreme cleanliness that almost bordered on the surreal. But beneath this polished exterior, it lacked the subtle yet crucial nuances of medical care I was accustomed to. The pain management, for instance, was inadequate. The idea of comfort seemed secondary to the goal of surgery. Did I mention that I didn't speak fluent Spanish either?

It wasn't an impulsive decision. It was an act of desperation, a hail mary pass, thrown in the hopes of a game-changer. I went to Tijuana alone. Friends and family thought I had lost my mind, believing the surgery to be a reckless gamble. With each mile that took me closer to Tijuana, I felt more alone. I wasn't merely crossing a geographical boundary; I was crossing a psychological threshold too. I was putting my life in the hands of strangers in a strange land, hoping for a miracle. It was a drastic measure, born out of desperation and fueled by a burning desire for change. Yet, amidst the fear and uncertainty, a tiny ember of hope flickered in my heart, pushing me forward.

When I returned to the States, my body betrayed me. A significant leak from the surgery site had created a life-threatening situation. My hospital room became my new home, where I would spend the ensuing two months grappling with life and death.

Fluid flooded my lungs, turning each breath into a Herculean struggle. I was only the second patient in the state who had been hospitalized with a similar issue. There was a chance I would not be healed enough to ever consume solid food again. Over fifteen procedures were conducted. Two stents were thrust into my tormented stomach in a desperate bid to heal an abscess, the aftermath of the stubborn leak. My nourishment came in the form of liquid food through ports, an irony not lost on me given that my initial motive was to control my relationship with food.

Life revolved around a strict regimen of pain medications and infectious disease drips. Two months felt like an eternity. From my hospital room, I watched people savor their coffee with friends at the café across the street, their joy tantalizingly out of reach. It was a simple act, yet it seemed like an extravagant luxury I may never have.

Yet, amidst this grim reality, I clung to hope. Surprisingly, I wasn't afraid. I knew that my higher powers had led me to the best doctors and nurses. My life was now in their hands, and I trusted that was exactly where I was supposed to be.

During a surgical procedure, my heart failed. I had died. My world receded into the silent shadows, a profound peace engulfing me. Suddenly, the brutal jolt of a defibrillator paddled me back to life. I woke up to a world of hurt, every muscle blazing with soreness as if I'd run a marathon and lifted every weight I could find. The nurses' faces lit up with relief when they saw me conscious. I was alive: battered, but unbroken. I still had a mission in life that was not completed. With every sore movement, my determination grew and, with death, an epiphany.

What I realized was that our society has built an image of 'perfection' that neither men nor women can live up to, and I had fallen prey to it. This unrealistic ideal has perpetuated a toxic culture of overwork, stress, and mental health issues. In our society, women are expected to be jugglers of roles - a loving wife, an attentive mother, a successful career woman, a meticulous homemaker, and above all, they are expected to look perpetually youthful and fit. The pervasiveness of this unrealistic expectation weighs heavily, creating a relentless pressure to 'have it all' and 'do it all'. The societal stereotype that insists on her playing all roles to perfection is not only unrealistic, but it's also fundamentally harmful.

This pressure confuses gender roles and expectations, creating a churning sea of confusion, disappointment, stress, and disillusionment. It creates a toxic environment of unattainable ideals, thereby fostering an environment ripe for mental health issues like depression and anxiety. Some of us even experience death in our pursuit of "doing it all".

The narrative that one individual, regardless of their gender, must check all the boxes of societal expectations is inherently flawed. It negates the concept of individuality and breeds an environment of relentless stress, self-doubt, and negative self-worth.

It's high time we embrace our authentic selves, acknowledge our struggles, and celebrate our individual journeys. We are not flawed for failing to meet these unrealistic expectations; instead, we are uniquely beautiful in our struggles, resilience, and journeys.

We need to strive for balance, acknowledge our limitations, and understand that we are human beings, not machines designed to fulfill endless societal expectations. It is essential to nurture our mental and emotional health, for they are just as vital as our physical well-being. To cultivate this balance, we need to prioritize self-care.

My harrowing journey and my brush with death served as a stark wake-up call. It was a profound realization of the fragility of life and the paramount importance of self-care. It spurred me to change my life's direction, steering me towards a path of healing and helping others.

The drastic measures I took to alter my body, the scars I bore, and the pain I endured led me to dig deeper and understand the complexities of mental health and nutrition. I dedicated myself to studying these fields and equipping myself with knowledge that could potentially save lives.

Today, I stand tall as an expert in mental health and nutrition. My thriving practice in hypnotherapy and nutritional counseling is a testament to my perseverance and my commitment to self-improvement. But it's more than just a career. It's my mission and my solemn vow that no woman should ever have to undergo the torment that I experienced.

Through hypnotherapy, I guide my clients to confront their deepest fears and anxieties, allowing them to heal from within. With nutritional counseling, I help them navigate the intricate world of food and diet, empowering them to make healthier choices.

This isn't just about weight loss or achieving an ideal body image.

It's about nurturing a healthy relationship with one's body and mind. It's about breaking the vicious cycle of self-loathing and guilt. It's about healing, growing, and learning to love oneself, imperfections and all.

Life is too precious to be squandered by societal pressures and unrealistic expectations. Let my story serve as a reminder that you are not alone and that you do not have to navigate your struggles alone. Reach out, seek help, and remember that it's okay to prioritize your well-being over societal norms. We all have our battles to fight, but with the right support, guidance, and a balanced approach to physical, mental, and emotional health, we can indeed thrive exactly as we were meant to.

Chapter Twenty-Eight
Setting the Stage for a Life of Fulfillment
By Melissa Trinci

M eet Melissa Trinci, a multi-talented mindset coach and entrepreneur, well-versed in many techniques, including Neuro-Linguistic Programming and the Trauma Healing Method. With a deep-rooted passion for empowering individuals, Melissa employs innovative techniques to help clients overcome self-limiting beliefs and behaviors. She has a particular expertise in aiding those who have faced challenges or traumas, and she works with a diverse clientele ranging from professionals to individuals seeking personal growth.

She excels in nurturing personal and professional growth across various domains, emphasizing the importance of leading a fulfilled life. A firm believer in the power of determination and hard work, Melissa is dedicated to guiding clients in carving out their path and fostering a legacy of healing, wealth, and wisdom for generations.

In addition to her coaching, Melissa is also a business savvy entrepreneur. She has successfully built Trinci Consulting Services, specializing in medical billing and credentialing, and Serenita Wellness, a platform for online therapy and holistic wellness. Her endeavors reflect her commitment to making a positive impact on individuals and the community at large.

www.linkedin.com/in/melissa-trinci

www.instagram.com/melissatrinci

www.facebook.com/mtrinci

www.melissatrinci.com

Setting the Stage for a Life of Fulfillment

By Melissa Trinci

In a world filled with a myriad of voices, promises, and dreams, let us pause for a moment. Close your eyes, take a deep breath, and ask yourself, "What does a fulfilling life mean to me?" Is it a life that embodies freedom, a sense of accomplishment, a never-ending thirst for learning, or a life that carries the mark of healing, growth, and encouragement? It's unique for each of us, yet there's something deeply shared in our quest for fulfillment.

To build a fulfilling life, we first need to understand our very foundation, what our deepest belief systems are, and uncover anything that will get in the way of moving in a new direction. Let's embark on a journey to uncover the layers of our minds, for there lies the cornerstone of our visions and dreams - the subconscious.

In this chapter, I will walk you through the basics of your subconscious mind, appreciating its role in our everyday life and understanding how to access it when we need to make changes to move forward.

Subconscious: The Foundation of Who We Are

Imagine your life as a building: this building, adorned with intricate designs, expansive rooms, and impressive features, has a story to tell. The foundation of this building must be solid. The foundation, the bedrock on which everything else rests, symbolizes your subconscious mind.

The subconscious mind operates as an astonishingly efficient processor, tirelessly managing an extensive array of information. Even when your focus is elsewhere, your subconscious is at work – modulating your heart rate, supervising respiratory patterns, and orchestrating many functions imperative for your well-being. But the prowess of the subconscious extends far beyond biological mechanics; it is also the storehouse of your life's narrative. It accumulates memories, emotions, and beliefs accrued over your lifetime concerning yourself, others, and the environment that surrounds you. Think of it as an intricately woven fabric, each thread representing a singular experience, belief, or emotion. These interwoven threads solidify into the very bedrock of your identity, continually shaping your responses and decisions.

Neural Adaptation: Rewiring Pathways for Change

Our brains consist of neural pathways – highways of information formed by our thoughts and beliefs. These pathways strengthen with repetition. Changing beliefs at the subconscious level involves rewiring these neural pathways, a phenomenon known as neuroplasticity – the brain's ability to adapt and change.

Now, let's talk about a fascinating part of our brain called the Reticular Activating System (RAS). The RAS acts as a filter for the overwhelming amount of information our brains receive daily. When we set intentions or change beliefs, we're essentially programming the RAS to bring to our attention things aligned with our new focus. This means by focusing on positive beliefs and reinforcing them, we're directing our brain to prioritize these newly-formed pathways, and our RAS helps in spotting opportunities and resources in sync with these new beliefs.

Techniques such as meditation, affirmations, and cognitive reframing can be employed to influence the subconscious mind and form empowering neural pathways. The key is to keep focusing on the positive, making these new pathways stronger and more dominant.

Journey to the Core: Addressing the Root of Belief Systems

To bring about a true transformation, it's necessary to address deep-seated belief systems rooted early in life, possibly due to influences from family, peers, or experiences. These beliefs might be so ingrained that surface-level affirmations cannot untangle them.

Consider a tree grown slanted due to the wind. That tree is all of us, and the winds are the influences and experiences that have continually shaped us. To straighten the tree, it's not enough to just prop it up. We need to nourish the roots and gradually allow it to regain strength.

Similarly, to truly change our belief systems, we need to dig deep and address the roots. We need to scrutinize what's beneath and discern the origin of our beliefs. Are they genuinely ours, or were they handed down from others' fears, prejudices, or limitations? It's only when we start this excavation that we can uncover these root belief systems and commence the real transformation work.

Remember, we are not only addressing the conscious mind but also reshaping the subconscious. Our subconscious mind, with its RAS, is a reliable assistant in this transformative journey. It helps us filter and focus on the positive, empowering beliefs we want to amplify, assisting us in rewiring our neural pathways for a more fulfilling life.

Visualization: The Catalyst for Change

Now, it's time to wield a powerful tool - visualization. Visualization is the art of creating compelling and vivid pictures in your mind. It's a form of mental rehearsal where you imagine your ideal life, complete with the dreams, goals, and lifestyle you desire. This practice makes your dreams more tangible and reinforces your belief in their feasibility.

Here's the magic: when you consistently visualize your desired outcomes, your subconscious mind begins to interpret these images as real experiences. Remember our friend, the RAS? It doesn't distinguish between real and imagined experiences. It views every mental image as actual data and aligns your thought process and behavior to match your imagined reality.

Consider this: elite athletes use visualization techniques to enhance their performance. They mentally rehearse the exact movements, emotions, and outcomes they want to achieve, training their subconscious to respond when it's game time. Visualization can work similarly for us in everyday life.

Through consistent visualization, we nurture our subconscious mind with imagery that matches our aspirations, helping to overwrite any limiting beliefs and reinforce the newly formed empowering neural pathways. The more vivid and engaging the visualization, the more influential it becomes.

This process serves as a bridge between our subconscious beliefs and conscious desires. It helps to align our deepest belief systems with our conscious aspirations, acting as a catalyst for bringing our imagined reality to fruition.

Navigating the Journey: Support and Guidance

Understanding and harnessing the power of our subconscious mind is pivotal in our quest for fulfillment. Our work entails refining our belief systems, rewiring our neural pathways, and employing practical tools like visualization. This concerted effort lays the groundwork for profound transformation. Remember, the journey to a fulfilling life begins in the fertile garden of our subconscious mind. When we acknowledge and cultivate this potent resource, we unlock limitless potential.

However, this journey is not always straightforward. We often find ourselves at crossroads, facing deep-rooted beliefs that are hard to untangle and even harder to alter. While traditional techniques can work wonders, there are times when they might not be enough.

We may try to plant roses in a garden filled with weeds, only to find our efforts fruitless. In such times, it's not a sign of failure but an indication that we need to dig deeper beneath the surface-level affirmations and visualizations.

This juncture is a calling to seek professional guidance. Life coaches, therapists, and guides are trained to help you navigate these complexities. They can assist in uncovering and addressing deep-seated belief systems that may not be accessible through conventional self-help strategies. Engaging with someone facilitating this deeper exploration can be a game-changer, providing the necessary tools and insights to unearth, understand, and ultimately reshape these entrenched patterns.

The Road Ahead: Unlocking Infinite Possibilities

By seeking help, you are not signifying weakness but displaying courage—the courage to face your innermost fears, limitations, and obstacles—the courage to change. As we embark on this journey, know that it is okay to seek support and to lean on others who can guide us towards our destination—a life that truly resonates with us. After all, the journey to self-realization and fulfillment is not meant to be walked alone.

We're all navigating our own paths, but none of us are alone. With dedication, support, and the right tools, we can all uncover our subconscious beliefs, reshape them, and ultimately manifest the fulfilling life we seek. Remember, the power to shape your life resides within you. It's a matter of unlocking it, understanding it, and making it work for you. Let's embark on this journey together.

With the right guidance and an understanding of your subconscious mind, the possibilities are infinite. Your fulfilling life awaits!

Chapter Twenty-Nine

A Vision for Living Your Best Life
By Kelsey Paasch

Through a tailored coaching program and personalized mentorship, Kelsey Paasch offers small business owners and key leaders invaluable insights, guidance, and strategies to navigate the complex landscape of leadership. Whether it's developing short and long-term business goals, implementing effective execution strategies, optimizing operational processes, or developing cohesive team cultures, Kelsey is committed to equipping leaders with the tools they need to succeed. With a customized and personal approach, Kelsey understands that each leader faces unique challenges and takes a holistic approach, considering the individual's aspirations, strengths, and areas for growth. By fostering an environment of trust and collaboration, Kelsey helps leaders gain clarity, develop resilience, and build the confidence necessary to overcome obstacles and achieve their goals.

With her guidance, support, and unwavering belief in your potential, you can confidently navigate the challenges of leadership and build a thriving business that reflects your unique vision and values.

www.linkedin.com/in/kelseypaasch
www.instagram.com/kelsey_e_paasch
www.facebook.com/Kelsey.E.Paasch
www.contourconsulting.co

A Vision for Living Your Best Life

By Kelsey Paasch

What is your vision for your life? Unknowingly or knowingly, we all have visions.

If you asked a group of people this question, you would hear a quick response with answers such as:

> *"I want to be happy."*
> *"I want to be healthy."*
> *"I want to retire early and travel."*
> *"I want to be successful in my career."*
> *"I want..." you fill in the blank.*

However, if you were to ask that same group of people whether they are currently living their envisioned life, most of them would probably admit that they are not.

So, what holds us back from living the life we desire?

In his book *The Power of One More*, Ed Mylett suggests that the limitations preventing us from living our vision arise from an inaccurate depth perception of how far that vision is from our current reality. He suggests that in the pursuit of our dreams, we unknowingly create obstacles that keep our goals at a distance through self-regulated behaviors and patterns in our everyday lives.

What if it really is as simple as removing ourselves from our own way?

Growing up, I was always told that my natural leadership, organizational skills, and personal ambitions would allow me to be a great leader. While I had no idea what that would look like, I knew that someday I would own my own business and help others by utilizing my skills.

From an early age, I put in hard work and dedication in every job

I took on, quickly assuming key leadership roles. By the time I turned 25, I had earned a college degree, married the love of my life, and was on the verge of a store leadership position with a prominent retail company. I was confident that the role was within reach, and I was told the final interviews were more of a formality. Unfortunately, the interview did not go the way I had planned, and I was informed that I could come back for another attempt in a few months.

Eventually, I did secure the position, but the lack of confidence from the initial failed interview haunted me for years. I began to doubt myself, leading to imitating other leaders instead of embracing my unique leadership style. Overthinking situations became a regular occurrence, causing tremendous stress when executing tasks, and the fear of failure consumed me with every decision I made. As time went on, I realized that I could not continue living in this constant state of stress. The long hours I spent away from my family disrupted the balance I sought to achieve. My growing dissatisfaction with my career paired with increasing demands on my time further fueled my desire for a change. With a second child on the way, and the pregnancy considered high-risk, I decided it was time to step away from my current path.

I spent the next year focusing on the health of our newest son and ensuring that my family was prioritized. While I enjoyed the time, I also knew that deep down, my desire to be in the working world was still there and that there had to be a way to balance both. Soon, an opportunity to join an online retailer in a key leadership role became available, and I was excited to jump back to work. However, old doubts resurfaced, challenging my credibility to hold such a position. The struggle to align work demands and family life continued, pulling me further from the vision I had for my life.

Five years later, our family welcomed our third child, and I found myself working in a smaller, local, family-owned company. Although the balance between work and family life was slightly better, I couldn't shake the feeling that I still wasn't fulfilling my true calling. A pivotal moment occurred during a heartfelt conversation with the

CEO when I considered sacrificing a family trip for a company-wide meeting. His sincerity struck a chord within me, as he reminded me that time with my children is precious and that work would always be there. It served as a powerful reminder that while work is constant, the moments we share with our loved ones are fleeting. During that family vacation, I took the time to reflect on what truly mattered in my vision for life and realized that I hadn't been prioritizing it as I should have. It was then that I resolved to turn my childhood dream into a reality.

As a child, I had no specific idea of the business I wanted to own, but after accumulating fifteen years of experience in high-leadership roles, my vision became clear. Drawing from both corporate and small business backgrounds, I recognized the need for sharing the valuable lessons, skills, and processes I had acquired.

As I reflect on my own journey, I've come to realize that I placed numerous limitations on my own vision. I allowed past failures and comparisons with others' achievements to overshadow the joy that comes from forging a unique path toward my vision. Now, armed with the knowledge I have gained, I am passionate about sharing my learnings and supporting fellow leaders in discovering their visions, crafting actionable plans, and ensuring their success in reaching their goals.

Through my strategic process, I empower my clients to take charge of their destiny, embrace their full potential, and live their vision with unwavering determination. The process is designed to be empowering, transformative, and adaptable, enabling individuals to thrive both personally and professionally as they embark on their path to growth and success. With this simple yet powerful framework in place, my clients can confidently navigate the challenges and opportunities that lie ahead, equipped with the knowledge and strategies needed to make their dreams a tangible reality.

Below is a simplified version of the process I use with my clients to strategize for their growth and success.

The initial phase is a Discover session where we delve into what is consuming your time and focus. This allows us to acknowledge your accomplishments, extend grace when we have taken on too much, and gain clarity on the work that lies ahead.

Activity:

Take a moment to assess your current state. Write down everything you are currently working on and responsible for. Identify where you are excelling, where you might be falling behind, and what tasks you haven't had the opportunity to begin. Reflect on both the positive and challenging aspects and write them down.

Next, we move on to the Strategize phase. Here, we focus on organizing, prioritizing, and planning the steps that will lead you toward your vision. During this session, we review the notes from the Discover phase and identify the top three to five priorities for the next three months. We then break down these priorities into four to six specific actionable tasks with designated due dates. This process helps you track your progress toward your ultimate goals.

Activity:

Refer to your Discover notes and select three to five key areas to focus on for the next three months. Once you've identified them, outline four to six tasks for each priority that will help you achieve those goals. Assign a target date for each task to ensure a clear plan for the upcoming three months.

Lastly, we proceed to the Succeed phase. This session centers around understanding the routines and behaviors crucial for keeping you on track with your three-month focuses. We discuss how you will measure your success, the support system you need to ensure achievement, and how to handle new ideas that may arise.

Activity:

As you review your plan up to this point, reflect on the routines and habits that will be vital for your success. Identify potential challenges that could hinder your progress. Consider the individuals who can support you in your journey and document their roles. Additionally, reserve space for great ideas that may not align with your current focuses. This will serve as a valuable idea bank for when you create your next three-month plan.

As you contemplate your unique journey, dare to deeply ponder your vision. Are the actions you are taking today aligned with that vision? If not, are you proactively devising a plan to manifest that vision? Remember, it is never too late to embark on that journey.

Craft YOUR vision and create a tailored plan to bring it to life. Don't allow anyone, not even yourself, to hinder you from living the life you truly desire.

Chapter Thirty

Affirming an Abundant Life
By Jennifer Kiser

Jennifer Kiser has experienced a passion for movement, nutrition, fitness, and wellness since she was a little girl. She was driven to lead friends, family, and community since the age of 6. As she looks back in time, she remember dreaming many dreams of becoming an icon for fitness, wellness, and leadership. She dreamed of performing and speaking to mass audiences, impacting millions. As a teenager, she began to lead fitness and nutrition classes to the community, and by the age of 18, she was leading stress-anxiety management courses, and became a certified fitness instructor, and speaker for incoming students at her college.

Advised to discontinue her journey due to lack of pay etc., but rather than listening to others, she followed her heart and pressed on. Today, she is a master of health science (Logan Chiropractic University), kinesiologist, exercise physiologist, master certified life coach (ICF), bodybuilder athlete and model, educational-motivational speaker with a focus of identity, trauma, self-esteem, body image, confidence. She is a nutrition consultant, performance coach, and neurolinguistic programming practitioner. She will continue to grow and develop in order to impact the community through her driven passion, forevermore. She has a passion to help others discover their identity and apply it to their life, in order to live the most optimal life dreamed or perceived!

www.linkedin.com/in/jennifer-kiser-816992230
www.instagram.com/jkmastercoaching
www.facebook.com/JenniferKiser

Affirming an Abundant Life

By Jennifer Kiser

When you think of the word *abundance*, what instantly comes to your mind? What does it mean to live a life of abundance? Abundance is defined as *the state or condition of possessing a copious quantity of something, such as prosperity or plentifulness.* Abundance is the opposite of scarcity and may be translated into sufficient wealth, health, love, fulfillment, wholeness, and spirituality. Abundance is *all-embracing.* When you are facing moments of heavy burden or feelings of being *stuck*, these are signs of contraction in mind, body, spirit.

Everyday women encounter a multitude of challenges as we proceed with the demands of today's culture. Feelings of self-doubt, negative thinking, coping with stress, burnout, dealing with setbacks, health issues, identity issues, and trauma-management are among a few barriers that everyday women experience. Accruing knowledge and consistent practice of the tools provided are keys to creating and affirming an abundant life.

Instead of passively waiting for good fortune to arrive, let's proceed with the belief that you are able to create a life of fulfilled abundance.

Key Factors to Creating an Abundant Life

- Expansion of Awareness
- Reduce and release the act and level of Futility
- Minimize Isolation
- Practice replacing Pessimistic thoughts into Optimistic action
- Take full Responsibility
- Create a clear-sighted Vision for your Life

Expansion of Awareness. When you are feeling overwhelmed, overburdened, anxiousness which has created an atmosphere in your mind of hopelessness, despair, heavy-burden, or stuck, these are indications of contraction of the mind, body, spirit. Setting aside quiet time in a place that is relaxed and allows stillness twice daily will allow expansion of awareness. Practicing meditation and allowing yourself to become grounded will allow your brain, body, mind, and spirit to recalibrate. Our brain is naturally designed to rebalance when we create time to be still. During this time of meditation, you may simply close your eyes and breathe, pray, stretch, visualize (e.g. ocean waves), feel, or smell a moment of joy.

Tips to Expand Life

- Be self-sufficient and take possession of everything in your life.
- Be passionate about your life and experiences.
- Remain open and accrue as much input as possible.
- Do not abandon the feedback loop with judgment, prejudices, and rigid beliefs.
- Do not censor incoming data through denial.
- Examine various points of view as if they were your own.
- Work on psychological blocks like shame and guilt; they falsely paint your reality.
- To be emotionally resilient is the best defense against growing rigid, so free yourself emotionally.
- Harbor no secrets; they create dark places in the psyche.
- Create willingness to redefine yourself daily.
- Do not regret the past or fear the future. Regret and fear bring misery through self-doubt.

Reduce and Release the Act and Level of Futility. Practice on avoiding the indulgence of the voice of futility. Although everyday women encounter a plethora of stress and burdens, controlling our thoughts of hopelessness, uselessness, emptiness, ineffectiveness, meaninglessness, and failure creates a downward spiral of thoughts and feelings. Firmly, yet gently, resist the persistence of these thoughts by creating thoughts of gratefulness and thankfulness into your mind. Continue to generate and reiterate thoughts/words of gratefulness, transforming thoughts directing into a healthy mindset. Remind yourself with gratitude, you are worthy; state the facts!

Minimize Isolation. Isolation may manufacture feelings detrimental to your emotional well-being and your state of mind. Signs that isolation is affecting your mental health are as follows: feelings of depression and anxiety, aggressive behavior, passive attitude, poor sleep quality, cognitive decline, altered memory, and poor self-care or self-neglect. Exercise connecting with groups of people who have undergone similar life experiences, for support. Personally, online "women's support" groups supported me tremendously during times of feeling isolated. Serving in the community, joining a faith-based group, reaching out to an old friend or neighbor are proactive methods to minimize isolation as well. Register for a new class, ask a coworker to introduce you to new people, learn something new, and/or create a list of things you would like to experience in life. Although everyone has the desire to preserve dignity and spare others of pain or loss, reaching out to the community and/or engaging in new experiences is a positive outlet to minimize isolation.

Practice Replacing Pessimistic Thoughts into Optimistic Action. The pessimist points to processes in which life has deteriorated, believing the worst will always happen. The optimist believes that the world is the best of all possibilities, is hopeful and confident about the future and success; good must ultimately prevail. Negative thoughts and actions may be replaced with positive thoughts and actions. Practicing the replacement of one negative behavior with a positive action daily will ultimately assist with the transition of pessimistic behavior to optimistic.

Practicing the Following Actions Will Aid With Optimistic Views

- Stand up for yourself
- Speak your truth
- Fix what can be fixed
- Ask for help
- Seek wise advice
- Walk away from things that can't be fixed
- Reduce the stress
- Look at your role in creating the negative situation

Small consistent action steps create positive transformation, thus an optimistic mindset.

Take Full Responsibility. Abundance comes from within, which means that taking full responsibility is a solution to reclaiming ownership of your life. Being responsible is the same as stepping into your own life journey and reclaiming ownership by stating the inescapable truth. Stating that you are a victim is a mindset that external forces are dictating your life, with the hope of a radical cure. Recognizing that situations only change when you accept the responsibility of your own life, good and bad, is the solution to *victim thinking*. Negative life occurrences have already entered your life, so create a positive outlook that aids with awareness, new discoveries, and solutions for your reclaimed future. Although managing responsibility for your thoughts, actions, and life can feel challenging, accepting ownership also builds grit, character, and self-respect.

Create a Clear-Sighted Vision for Your Life. Have you ever witnessed a person who is rich, but miserable? Although material abundance is useful, it falls short of creating a sense of fulfillment. Fulfillment is generated through heightened senses of awareness, manifesting a vision of purpose for your life. Dreams create visions, visions create focus, focus creates discipline. The higher the vision, the greater you will feel fulfilled through a deeper level of awareness. Cultivate your vision and perspective, apply logic and planning, and allow your vision to flow through practical application of your vision. Once you have envisioned and confirmed your deepest desires, begin your journey of action. Your identity, life, and visions are yours to acknowledge and protect. No one is allowed to rob you of your visions, your purpose, your life, without your consent. Live abundantly!

Although everyday women encounter a multitude of challenges as we proceed with the demands of today's culture, we have the power to gain back control of our thoughts and actions. The feelings of self-doubt, negative thinking, coping with stress, burnout, dealing with setbacks, health issues, identity issues, and trauma-management will be resolved through the "life of abundance" mindset. Let's cultivate accruing knowledge and consistent practice of the tools provided to create and affirm an abundant life.

Instead of passively waiting for good fortune to arrive, let's proceed with the belief that you are able to discover a life of fulfilled abundance!

I Am~

Chapter Thirty-One

From Brokenness to Inner Victory
by Tricia Taylor-Shipley

Tricia Taylor-Shipley is your "Never Too Late Ambassador" and Soul Connection founder.

She empowers women in their midlife who yearn for more, but find themselves trapped in their comfort zone, feeling adrift, under-valued, and frequently encased in a sense of despair. She purpose is to guide them to self-discovery, boost confidence, and enable them to shine, irrespective of age. Her passionately believes being over 50 heralds exciting adventures and she's here to provide a boarding pass to freedom.

A survivor of fear, imposter syndrome, and business failures, she has harnessed these experiences to create a platform for assisting women struggling with their self-worth. On the mystical ReOrient Express, she provides tools to break mediocrity and fearlessly embrace potential. In her world, age is just a number, and it's never too late to embrace one's true self and live the life you've always dreamt of.

www.linkedin.com/in/tricia-taylorshipley
www.instagram.com/journeywithSoulConnection
www.facebook.com/soulconnection.me
www.soulconnection.uk

From Brokenness to Inner Victory

by Tricia Taylor-Shipley

I was once a name lost in the shadows. I was born into a world of humble beginnings, where dreams and desires coexisted amidst the struggles of everyday life. My name had little significance, but a yearning for a better life burned deep within me. The modest coal-fuelled fire provided physical warmth, but it couldn't chase away the nagging feeling of inadequacy.

Unbeknownst to me, this feeling was more than fleeting; it had become deeply ingrained and had seeped into my veins like poison. I had unwittingly become captive to seeking validation from external sources and relying heavily on material possessions to define my value. This twisted belief echoed relentlessly in my mind, casting a haunting shadow over every aspect of my life. My constant habit of comparing myself to others left me totally dissatisfied with my life.

Over the years, the weight of my unfulfilled dreams grew heavy, leading me down a path of catastrophic decision making. However, one Sunday afternoon, fate intervened.

As I walked along a lane, there, hidden behind some large trees, stood an imposing house that I hadn't noticed before. Upon closer inspection, I could sense the house's silent plea for care and attention. Its once-grand sash windows were veiled by closed venetian blinds, shutting out the light, as if shielding itself from the world. As I gazed upon the forlorn house, with its tightly closed shutters, I recognized a profound reflection of my own hidden insecurities—deep-seated inadequacies that I had silently harboured throughout most of my life. But, despite its need for some TLC, it still had a unique beauty that attracted me and I turned to my partner and said, "Oh, I would love to live there."

My partner's response cut through my daydream, "you can - in your dreams." And so, the house existed in the recesses of my mind for the next two years. Until one fateful day, a new "For Sale" sign appeared. I immediately saw an opportunity—a chance to finally possess something unique, something that would symbolize achievement, stability, and security, and this was it, this house was a dream come true.

But dreams can sometimes turn bittersweet, and so it was for me. With great anticipation, my partner and I moved into the house, and I poured my heart and soul into making it a home. In my eyes, it became more than just a house; it became a symbol of my self-esteem, a source of pride and fulfilment. The bricks and mortar affirmed my worthiness. Finally, I believed I had found the key to my significance. As the house transformed, so did I. The empty longing that had driven me for so long gradually gave way to a deeper sense of self-acceptance and inner fulfilment.

Yet, life has a way of upending our plans, and unexpected twists and turns shattered my fragile illusion of stability. Tragedy struck when my partner passed away from a heart attack at the age of 49 years. The future we had envisioned together vanished, along with the last beat of his heart, leaving me adrift in a sea of loss and uncertainty.

For three long and agonizing years, my life felt like an aimless journey through a desolate wilderness. But then, in the midst of my vulnerability and emotional turmoil, a flicker of light emerged from the darkness. I met someone new, someone who seemed to hold the promise of filling the void that consumed me.

However, what began as a beacon of hope soon turned into a nightmare of unimaginable proportions. After 18 months, I found myself entangled in a legal battle that would stretch on for four years. It became a merciless duel, a fight for survival against an adversary determined to dismantle every aspect of my life.

The weight of the legal dispute bore down on me, crushing my spirit and leaving me utterly devastated. The walls of my cherished home, once filled with warmth and love, echoed with my fear, as I faced the prospect of losing it. And so it was, my intangible pillar of self-worth was ruthlessly stripped away, leaving me feeling exposed and vulnerable.

The pain became suffocating and, in search of solace, I made the impulsive decision to accept a job opportunity in Bangladesh. I believed that leaving behind the remnants of my shattered life would bring respite from the torment that plagued me.

So there I was. My belongings were all in storage and I was going to Bangladesh. I should have been excited at what lay ahead, but my heart was broken. I had lost my beautiful home. I had lost everything and I wanted to get away from the memories, the hurt, the pain, and most of all, the humiliation and shame.

As I closed the heavy oak doors of my beloved house, tears streamed down my face in torrents, each drop a testament to the profound loss I had endured. The pain was unbearable and, with a heavy heart, I walked towards my car, my body wracked with sobs, feeling broken in every conceivable way.

My car slowly rolled down the drive, until it carried me out of sight of the house I had fallen in love with all those years ago. I couldn't look back. My heart felt like it was ripping out of my chest; each beat was a reminder of the deep wounds I carried. The chapter of my life in that house had come to a close, yet turning the page seemed impossible.

Fast forward to my new life and I soon discovered that physical distance also could not erase the deep-rooted hurt, pain, and shame that clung to me like a relentless shadow. Bangladesh, with its vibrant colours and rich culture, offered a temporary respite from the ghosts that haunted me but, within, the lack of self-worth remained, silently suffocating my spirit. After two years, plagued by illness and an over-whelming longing for my family, I made the arduous journey back home to England, my suitcases filled with remnants of a shattered life.

It was from this place of rock bottom, from the confines of a small bedroom in my daughter's home, that I embarked on a desperate search to rediscover the fragments of the old Patricia—the one who once held hopes and dreams. Many nights were spent, tears mingling with fervent prayers for strength and courage to keep moving forward. Despite the depths of despair, a faint spark persisted within me, a spark I had felt since childhood—a whisper of resilience and determination that refused to be extinguished.

Drawing upon my psychological knowledge acquired through years of study, and the wisdom gleaned from countless books that had nourished my soul, I resolved to turn my life around. With a glimmer of hope, my journey led me to the enchanting Scottish Highlands, a place renowned for its serene landscapes and untamed wilderness. There, in the embrace of nature's grandeur, I was forced to confront the truth—my truth.

Amidst the sweeping vistas and the majestic peaks and valleys of the Highlands, I began to grasp the significance of my story, and the immense power that resided within me. The breathtaking beauty mirrored the highs and lows of my own life—the moments of triumph and heartbreak, joy and sorrow. It was in those moments of introspection that I realized my worth transcended the confines of the house I had lost, and the possessions that had once defined me. True self-worth was not about seeking external validation; it lay within the depths of my soul.

I understood, with unwavering clarity, that my worth was rooted in my ability to love and be loved, to show kindness and empathy to others, and to embrace the unique gifts that resided within me. In the end, it was never the house that defined me, but the emotions and beliefs woven into the tapestry of my journey.

As I continue to walk this path of self-discovery, I do so with a renewed sense of purpose and compassion. The journey is ongoing, the road winding and uncertain, but I embrace it wholeheartedly, for I now know I am travelling on my own life train and heading towards my chosen destination.

I've found that the real magic for a flourishing life lies in unlocking our own inner strength. So why not treat yourself to a first-class ticket for a journey of self-discovery, and say goodbye to the ordinary? Witness as your life's journey transports you to places beyond your wildest dreams!

As you undertake this voyage, be prepared to face hurdles and unexpected twists. But keep in mind, every roadblock is an opportunity to build resilience. Embrace these challenges, as they are the gateway to the most captivating moments of your life.

This voyage is a chance to dive deep and discover what lies within. Remember, your journey is deeply personal. There's no need to rush, relish every transformative moment. After all, life isn't a sprint, but a journey meant to be savoured.

Chapter Thirty-Two

The Best Is Yet to Come
By Nicole Toney

Nicole Toney is a dedicated professional with a passion for personal development and education. She holds a Master's degree in Psychology and a Bachelor's degree in Human Resource Management, showcasing her commitment to both the human psyche and effective organizational management.

With a diverse background, Nicole has worn many hats in her career journey. Her experience spans from her early days as a public school teacher, where she helped shape young minds, to her roles as a corporate trainer, guiding individuals and organizations towards success. Nicole's expertise in Human Resources has equipped her with the skills to navigate the complexities of workforce management, ensuring that people are at the heart of every organization's success. Her work as a mental health case manager further reflects her dedication to the well-being of others.

Beyond her professional life, Nicole is a multifaceted individual. She finds joy in the simple pleasures of life, such as reading, cooking, and traveling, which not only enrich her experiences but also allow her to connect with different cultures and perspectives. Most importantly, she cherishes spending quality time with her family, where she finds love and inspiration.

As an entrepreneur, business consultant, life coach, and mentor, Nicole Toney continues to make a positive impact in both the corporate world and the lives of those she guides. Her unwavering commitment to personal growth and her genuine passion for helping others achieve their full potential define her as a truly inspirational figure.

ndtoney@gmail.com

www.facebook.com/profile.php?id=100084066543648&mibex
tid=haYZDX

www.linkedin.com/in/nicoledtoney

The Best Is Yet to Come

By Nicole Toney

Life isn't scripted and there are definitely lots of unknowns, but being flexible can help you navigate your way through. Change isn't easy, but it's necessary. It's better to accept changes that must be made and try to find the positives. By being more accepting of changes, we eliminate undue stress and frustration.

When we're young, we're trying to figure out who we are, who we want to be, and how we're going to get there. As we become adults, we're trying to figure out life and find where we fit. Once we are nearing middle age, we are usually at a pretty good place as far as maturity knowing what we want and how to get there. With maturity brings more focus and intentional thinking, allowing us to achieve the goals we've set for ourselves.

Yet, sometimes we still prioritize others over ourselves. To change this, we have to figure out what's important and what isn't. Ask yourself this question: "How can I truly love someone else if I really don't love myself?"

For years, I poured so much into everyone around me, it left nothing for myself. I almost didn't have an identity. I was a wife, a mom, an employee... but I didn't know who I really was. I didn't know what I liked to eat, places I wanted to go, or things I wanted to do, but I knew exactly what my husband and kids liked to eat and what they liked to do. It's okay to be selfish and focus on your needs and wants. Many times, we put what we need or want on the back burner in an effort to please others. Yes, you should handle your business and take care of what needs to be done in your life and those you are responsible for, but there should be times when you do something just for you. Remember that you can't give what you don't have. Oftentimes, we pour so much of ourselves into someone or something that there's nothing left for us.

Consider the source of any information you are receiving, whether it be advice, gossip, or just a simple conversation. It's a good habit to always consider, ponder, and even fact-check information before buying into it. It's good to consider the things or lessons people are trying to teach you, but ultimately you have to decide what's best for you.

Pray for discernment. Discernment is very useful in filtering out the people or things that won't bring anything good into your life. When you have discernment, you will be able to distinguish between good and bad. It's almost like a feeling or vibe you'll get that will let you know if something is right or wrong. When you have discernment, people won't be able to cause you as much frustration, pain, drama, or sadness. Yes, you will still experience these things, but to a lesser extent.

Dressing up for no reason, smiling often, and laughing out loud will help you feel better, even when everything in your life is not good. Remember the saying "fake it 'til you make it"? It really works. It's basically about putting your game face on like everything is okay, even when it's not. There have been times when I've felt lost and unloved, but I was able to dig down deep to keep pushing through so that I wouldn't get stagnant. Remember that slow is okay, just don't ever stop moving forward.

Don't allow people's opinion of you to be the end-all be-all. We can become insecure, unmotivated, and have low self-esteem based on the words or actions of others. Instead of allowing others' words to hurt us, we should use them to do some self-reflection, making improvements as needed and fueling us to be the best version of ourselves. Your words have power: speak positive affirmations over your life and your loved ones. Negative begets more negative. Positivity is empowering, while negativity is draining.

Peace of mind is priceless, never allow anyone to take that away. If you don't have peace of mind now, fight like crazy to get it, and fight like crazy to keep it. This can mean letting go of negative friends, leaving bad relationships, changing jobs or careers, or maybe just getting a hobby. Embrace the people in your life that shower you with unconditional love and honesty. Yes, the truth hurts sometimes, but it's always better than a lie. Stop running from the truth; look in the mirror and face it head on.

I spent many years of my life being angry about things that were out of my control. As I matured, I learned to not allow other people to dictate my happiness. I found out that trying to please everyone wasn't what was pleasing to me; I was unhappy trying to make others happy. Now I embrace my knowledge and common sense to do things in life that make me happy, things that will help elevate me, things that will help build my future, and things that will make me a better person. It's very important to find strength from something or someone in your life that will serve as fuel to drive you. What I mean by this is: what motivates you to get up every morning, or what motivates you to go to work everyday? This can be your children, your future goals, your family, retirement, etc.

Never let anyone tell you that you can't have it all, because you definitely can. You don't have to sacrifice having a family for a career or anything else. You can have anything you set out to achieve, whether it's a career, kids, spouse, house, or entrepreneurship, you can have it all.

Don't be afraid to press the reset button. Sometimes in life you have to stop everything; stop paying for the place you can't afford to live in, stop the relationship that's taking a toll on your mental health, stop paying for a car that keeps breaking down, and stop chasing people, forcing them to be in your life. If you don't press the reset button yourself, life will do it automatically; the car will get repossessed, you will get evicted from your residence, or you act out at work and get fired. I'm not saying that it's okay not to pay your bills or to be irresponsible, but if you're drowning sometimes the only way to save yourself is to get out of the water.

Don't be afraid of failure because those are lessons we need to strengthen us. It doesn't matter if you fall down as long as you get up, dust yourself off, and keep moving. Others may laugh at your efforts, but don't worry about them because you have a plan. Keep working your plan and only change courses if you deem it necessary, because everyone won't have your vision so don't try to force them to see it. The journey you are traveling is yours, so be wise when allowing others to join you.

Starting today, choose yourself and your happiness. Make sure you are being responsible for handling your business at home, work, and in the community, but always remember to make time for yourself. Having all of the money in the world means nothing if you're unhappy. You should continue to learn, grow, and evolve without being afraid to experience things that are new or different from what you're used to. Practice forgiving others, not to make them feel better, but because it will allow you to heal and move on. Spend time with loved ones, take time for yourself, and focus on being the best version of yourself that you can be. Remember, the best is yet to come!

Thank You

We want to thank you, dear reader, for taking time to read this. If you found these stories helpful please take a moment tto leave a review on Amazon.com **amzn.to/3rsJcbG** or Goodreads.com

Other Everyday Woman's Guide Books

Everyday Woman: All About You

By Galit Ventura-Rozen and Angela Giles

Everyday Woman's Guide to Doing What You Love:

51 Stories from Purpose Driven Women

Everyday Woman's Guide to Success in Your Business:

27 Stories from Successful Women

Everyday Woman's Guide to The Mindset Of A Successful Woman: 39 Stories from Successful Women

About Red Thread Publishing

Red Thread Publishing is an all-female publishing company on a mission to support 10,000 women to become successful published authors and thought leaders. Through the transformative work of writing and telling our stories we are not only changed as individuals, but we are also changing the global narrative & thus the world.

www.redthreadbooks.com

See our catalog of books:
bit.ly/RedThreadLibrary

f facebook.com/redthreadpublishing

instagram.com/redthreadbooks

Made in the USA
Monee, IL
29 October 2023

45410736R00152